The
Group Therapy
Treatment Planner

PRACTICE *PLANNERS*™ SERIES

Treatment *Planners*

The Child & Adolescent Psychotherapy Treatment Planner
The Chemical Dependence Treatment Planner
The Continuum of Care Treatment Planner
The Couples Psychotherapy Treatment Planner
The Employee Assistance Treatment Planner
The Pastoral Counseling Treatment Planner
The Older Adult Psychotherapy Treatment Planner
The Complete Adult Psychotherapy Treatment Planner, 2e
The Behavioral Medicine Treatment Planner
The Mental Retardation and Developmentally Disabled Treatment Planner
The Severely and Persistently Mentally Ill Treatment Planner
The Group Therapy Treatment Planner
The Child Psychotherapy Treatment Planner, 2e
The Adolescent Psychotherapy Treatment Planner, 2e
The Gay and Lesbian Psychotherapy Treatment Planner
The Neuropsychological Treatment Planner

Homework *Planners*

Brief Therapy Homework Planner
Brief Couples Therapy Homework Planner
Chemical Dependence Treatment Homework Planner
Brief Child Therapy Homework Planner
Brief Adolescent Therapy Homework Planner

Documentation *Sourcebooks*

The Clinical Documentation Sourcebook
The Forensic Documentation Sourcebook
The Psychotherapy Documentation Primer
The Chemical Dependence Treatment Documentation Sourcebook
The Clinical Child Documentation Sourcebook
The Couple and Family Clinical Documentation Sourcebook
The Clinical Documentation Sourcebook, 2e
The Continuum of Care Clinical Documentation Sourcebook

The Group Therapy Treatment Planner

Kim Paleg

Arthur E. Jongsma, Jr.

JOHN WILEY & SONS, INC.

New York • Chichester • Weinheim • Brisbane • Singapore • Toronto

I dedicate this book to Jim Voetberg, my group therapy partner when we were both just learning to listen, support, confront, teach, and affirm.

Arthur E. Jongsma, Jr.

To the clients in groups everywhere who have shared the wealth of their experience and made this book possible.

Kim Paleg

This book is printed on acid-free paper.∞

Copyright © 2000 by Kim Paleg and Arthur E. Jongsma, Jr. All rights reserved.
Published by John Wiley & Sons, Inc.
Published simultaneously in Canada.

All references to diagnostic codes and the entire content of Appendix B are reprinted with permission from the Diagnostic and Statistical Manual of Mental Disorders, Fourth Edition. Copyright 1994. American Psychiatric Association.

No part of this publication may be reproduced, stored in a retrieval system or transmitted in any form or by any means, electronic, mechanical, photocopying, recording, scanning or otherwise, except as permitted under Sections 107 or 108 of the 1976 United States Copyright Act, without either the prior written permission of the Publisher, or authorization through payment of the appropriate per-copy fee to the Copyright Clearance Center, 222 Rosewood Drive, Danvers, MA 01923, (978) 750-8400, fax (978) 750-4744. Requests to the Publisher for permission should be addressed to the Permissions Department, John Wiley & Sons, Inc., 605 Third Avenue, New York, NY 10158-0012, (212) 850-6011, fax (212) 850-6008, E-Mail: PERMREQ @ WILEY.COM.

This publication is designed to provide accurate and authoritative information in regard to the subject matter covered. It is sold with the understanding that the publisher is not engaged in rendering professional services. If legal, accounting, medical, psychological or any other expert assistance is required, the services of a competent professional person should be sought.

Designations used by companies to distinguish their products are often claimed as trademarks. In all instances where John Wiley & Sons, Inc. is aware of a claim, the product names appear in initial capital or all capital letters. Readers, however, should contact the appropriate companies for more complete information regarding trademarks and registration.

Library of Congress Cataloging-in-Publication Data

Paleg, Kim.
    The group therapy treatment planner / Kim Paleg and Arthur E. Jongsma, Jr.
        p.   cm. — (Practice planners series)
    ISBN 0-471-25468-1 (pbk./disk : alk. paper). — ISBN 0-471-25469-X
(pbk. : alk. paper)
    1. Group psychotherapy. I. Jongsma, Arthur E., 1943–   .
II. Title. III. Series: Practice planners.
RC488.P35   1999
616.89'152—dc21   99-16343
                                                                      CIP

Printed in the United States of America.

10 9 8 7 6 5 4 3 2 1

CONTENTS

PREFACE

The Group Therapy Treatment Planner was conceived as a way to facilitate the treatment of specific therapeutic problems in the group setting. At a time when managed care organizations are becoming the norm in health care and mental health benefits are being severely restricted, there is enormous pressure to treat problems in as cost-effective a way as possible. Focal group therapy is an effective, cost-reducing alternative to individual therapy.

Focal groups, in contrast to more traditional transference-based models of group therapy, are characterized by their homogeneity, their high degree of structure, their goal orientation, and their high educational function. Most are time-limited, though in this *Planner* the specific length of each group is left up to the individual clinician to determine. Also left up to the individual clinician are the issues of group size and the specific screening procedures she or he will use in determining eligibility for the group, apart from meeting the behavioral definitions listed for each specific problem.

Because most problems encountered in life are problems of relationships with others, from the family to the workplace to social activities, dealing with specific problems in the group format allows clients to work on their issues in the mode that often feels most familiar and comfortable to them. In a group setting, client problems can be acted out directly, as opposed to symbolically, and thus addressed more effectively. Furthermore, group members can share their resources and their insights and develop new self-perceptions along the way as they see themselves interacting in different ways.

The Group Therapy Treatment Planner outlines many treatment issues, the specific goals for treating them, and a range of eclectic interventions for reaching those goals. It is important to remember, however, that this treatment planner cannot substitute for either good clinical training and judgment or experience with groups. Both criteria must be met in order for the material in this book to be most effectively used.

On a personal note, I am grateful to Art Jongsma for his guidance and feedback; to his right-hand woman Jen Byrne for her uncomplaining approach to the difficulties incurred by my inability to bring my technological skills up to scratch; to my editor at John Wiley & Sons, Kelly Franklin, for her encouragement and support; and to the scores of colleagues who are doing terrific work with groups and from whose experience I drew in writing this book. Last but not least, I would like to thank my husband, who patiently guided me through my introduction to Windows and the electronic age of e-mail, and my children, who put up with late pickups, hastily thrown-together meals on writing days, and Saturday disappearances when writing days did not suffice.

—KIM PALEG, PH.D.

INTRODUCTION

Formalized treatment planning has become an essential component of mental health service delivery in the 1990s. To meet the standards of the Joint Commission on Accreditation of Healthcare Organizations (JCAHO), and to help clients qualify for third-party reimbursement, mental health professionals must develop treatment plans that are specific regarding problem definitions and interventions, and measurable in terms of setting milestones that can be used to chart progress. In conducting group therapy, treatment plans are no less important; group leaders as well as group members must be very clear about what they are attempting to attain in the group and how to determine whether those goals and objectives are in fact achieved. The purpose in writing this book, therefore, is to clarify, simplify, improve, and accelerate the group therapy treatment planning process.

TREATMENT PLAN UTILITY

Detailed, measurable, written treatment plans can benefit not only the clients, but also the therapist, the treatment team, the treatment agency, the insurance community, and even the entire mental health profession. The clients are served by a written plan because it clearly delineates the issues that are the focus of their treatment group. It is very easy for both the therapist and the group members to get stuck in the sharing of personal stories and lose sight of what they are hoping to attain. The treatment plan is a guide that structures the focus of the therapeutic contract. Because groups are made up of different mixes of people, each with their own particular version of the general issues, the treatment plan must be viewed as a dynamic document that will be updated to reflect major changes in emphasis as they occur. While recognizing that the plan may evolve throughout treatment, it nevertheless remains important to settle on specific treatment goals at the outset. Behaviorally based, measurable objectives clearly focus the treatment endeavor and provide a means of measuring treatment outcome. Clear objectives also allow the clients to channel their efforts into specific changes leading to the long-term goal of problem resolution.

Therapists are aided by treatment plans because they are forced to think analytically and critically about which interventions are best suited for a particular set of group therapy participants. In multi-provider settings, treatment plans not only help to clarify objectives but also serve the important function of delineating which clinician is responsible for which intervention. By providing a common language, *The Group Therapy Treatment Planner* can facilitate consistent and clear communication between members of the treatment team and with the clients.

Clinicians also benefit from clear documentation of treatment because it provides a measure of added protection from possible client litigation. Malpractice suits are increasing in frequency, and insurance premiums are soaring. The first line of defense against allegations is a complete clinical record detailing the treatment process. A written, formal treatment plan that has been reviewed and signed by each client and is accompanied by complete progress notes is a powerful defense against false claims.

Finally, the psychotherapy profession as a whole stands to benefit from the use of more precise, measurable objectives to evaluate success in mental health treatment. With the advent of detailed treatment plans, outcome data, particularly concerning the efficacy of group therapy compared with individual therapy, can be more easily collected for interventions that are effective in achieving specific goals.

HOW TO DEVELOP A TREATMENT PLAN

The process of developing a treatment plan involves logical steps that build on one another. The foundation of any effective treatment plan is the data gathered in a thorough biopsychosocial assessment. As the clients present themselves for inclusion in a group, the therapist must listen sensitively to discern where their struggles lie—in terms of family-of-origin issues, current stressors, emotional status concerns, social network pressures, physical health problems, coping skills, interpersonal conflicts, and so on. Assessment data may be gathered from such diverse sources as social histories, physical exams, clinical interviews, psychological tests, and genograms. The integration of this data by the therapist or the multidisciplinary treatment team is critical for understanding the client's individual issues and their dynamics as a member of a therapy group. Once the assessment is complete, use the following six steps to develop a treatment plan.

Step One: Problem Selection

This *Group Therapy Treatment Planner* offers treatment plan components for 28 problems most effectively dealt with in the group setting. For the most part, clients presenting themselves for participation in a specific group are clear about the problems they experience that make them appropriate candidates for that group. Sometimes a client may present with problems that could be adequately addressed in more than one group; at these times the therapist needs to determine whether the presenting problem is in fact the primary issue or whether another more pressing issue needs to be addressed more immediately. An effective group treatment plan can be applied only to a somewhat homogeneous population with a specific problem in common.

Step Two: Problem Definition

To lead a focal group, a therapist must decide on a specific problem focus and include as group members only those clients meeting specific behavioral criteria. Because each client presents for group treatment with unique nuances regarding how a particular problem manifests itself in his or her life, it's essential for the therapist to use clinical judgment in screening out clients whose problems don't sufficiently overlap those of the other group members. Symptoms of clients included in the group should be associated with diagnostic criteria and codes such as those found in the *Diagnostic and Statistical Manual* (DSM) or the *International Classification of Diseases. The Group Therapy Treatment Planner,* following the pattern established by DSM-IV, offers an array of behaviorally specific problem definition statements. Each of the 28 presenting problems has several behavioral symptoms from which to choose. These prewritten definitions may also be used as models in crafting additional definitions.

Step Three: Goal Development

The next step in treatment plan development is to set broad goals for the resolution of the target problem. These statements need not be crafted in measurable terms, but instead should focus on the long-term global outcomes of treatment. In writing long-term goals, it is important to remember the chosen time span of the specific therapy group being treated and to write goals that realistically reflect the allotted time. Although the *Planner* suggests several possible goal statements for each problem, it is not necessary to have more than one statement for a particular treatment plan.

Step Four: Objective Construction

In contrast to long-term goals, objectives must be stated in behaviorally measurable language. It must be clear when group members have achieved the established objectives. Review agencies (e.g., JCAHO), HMOs, and managed care organizations insist that treatment results be measurable. The objectives presented in *The Group Therapy Treatment Planner* are designed to meet this demand for accountability. Numerous alternatives are presented to allow construction of a variety of treatment plan possibilities for the same presenting problem. The therapist must exercise professional judgment about which objectives are most appropriate for a particular group of clients.

Each objective should be developed as a step toward attaining the broad treatment goal(s). In essence, objectives can be thought of as a series of steps that, when completed, will result in the achievement of the long-term goal. Given that even a fairly homogeneous group contains many different permutations of the same problem, there will necessarily be more objectives than might be necessary for individual clients in order to facilitate every group member achieving the desired goal. New objectives may be added to the plan as the group progresses. Achieving all the necessary objectives should signify resolution of group members' problems and attainment of the written long-term goal(s).

Step Five: Intervention Creation

Interventions are actions by the therapist designed to help group members achieve the objectives. There should be at least one intervention for every objective. If members do not accomplish the objective after the initial intervention, new interventions should be added to the plan.

Interventions should be selected on the basis of group members' needs and the therapist's full treatment repertoire. This *Group Therapy Treatment Planner* contains interventions from a broad range of therapeutic approaches, including cognitive, behavioral, dynamic, pharmacological, family systems, experiential/expressive, and solution-focused brief therapy. Other interventions may be written by the therapist to reflect his or her own training and experience.

Some suggested interventions listed in the *Planner* refer to specific books that can be assigned to group members for adjunctive bibliotherapy. Appendix A contains a full bibliographic reference list of these materials and others. The books are arranged under each problem for which they are appropriate as assigned reading for group members.

Step Six: Diagnosis Determination

The determination of an appropriate diagnosis for a particular group member is based on an evaluation of that member's complete clinical presentation in the group. The therapist must compare the behavioral, cognitive, emotional, and interpersonal symptoms presented by that client in the group to the criteria for diagnosis of a mental illness as described in DSM-IV. Careful assessment of behavioral indicators facilitates more accurate diagnosis.

HOW TO USE THIS PLANNER

Learning the skills of effective treatment plan writing can be a tedious and difficult process for many therapists. *The Group Therapy Treatment Planner* was developed as a tool to aid therapists in quickly writing treatment plans that are clear, specific, and customized to the particular needs of a group therapy population. Treatment plans should be developed by moving in turn through each of the following steps:

Choose the presenting problem (Step One) that you plan to use as the focus of a therapy group. Locate the corresponding page number for that problem in *The Group Therapy Treatment Planner*'s table of contents. Determine the optimal number of participants required for conducting this group.

Select two or three (or more) of the listed behavioral definitions (Step Two) and record them in the appropriate section on the treatment plan form.

Select at least one long-term goal (Step Three) and record it in the Goals section of the treatment plan form.

Review the listed objectives for this problem and select the ones clinically indicated for the population represented in the group (Step Four). Because groups consist of many different permutations of the same problem, it will probably be necessary to have several objectives to ensure achievement of goals for all members. Determine the length of the group necessary to achieve the chosen objectives.

Choose relevant interventions (Step Five). *The numbers of the interventions most salient to each objective are listed in parentheses following the objective statement.* Feel free to choose other interventions from the list or to add new interventions as needed in the space provided.

DSM-IV diagnoses that are commonly associated with the problem are listed at the end of each chapter. These diagnoses are suggestions for clinical consideration. For a particular group member, select a diagnosis listed or assign a more appropriate choice from the DSM-IV (Step Six).

Note: To accommodate those practitioners who tend to plan treatment in terms of diagnostic labels rather than presenting problems, Appendix B lists all of the DSM-IV diagnoses that are included in the *Planner,* cross-referenced to the problems related to each diagnosis.

Following these steps will facilitate the development of complete treatment plans, ready for immediate implementation and presentation to the group. The final plan should resemble an expanded (particularly with respect to objectives and interventions) version of the sample plan presented on the following pages.

ELECTRONIC TREATMENT PLANNING

As paperwork mounts, more and more therapists are turning to computerized record keeping. The presenting problems, goals, objectives, interventions, and diagnoses in *The Group Therapy Treatment Planner* are available in electronic form as an add-on upgrade module to the popular software *TheraScribe 3.0 for Windows: The Computerized Assistant to Treatment Planning* and *TheraScribe 3.5 for Windows.* For more information on *TheraScribe* or *The Group Therapy* add-on modules, call John Wiley & Sons at 1-800-879-4539, or mail the information request coupon at the back of this book.

A WORD OF CAUTION

Whether using the print *Planner* or the electronic version (*TheraScribe*), it is critical to remember that effective treatment planning requires that each plan be tailored to the needs of the specific population of clients in that group. Treatment plans should not be mass-produced, even when running the same kind of group again. The strengths and weaknesses of each particular group of clients, with their unique stressors and interactional patterns, must be considered in developing a treatment strategy. The clinically derived statements in this *Planner* can be combined in many ways to develop detailed treatment plans. In addition, readers are encouraged to add their own definitions, goals, objectives, and interventions to the existing samples.

SAMPLE TREATMENT PLAN

PROBLEM: ANGER CONTROL

Definitions: Overreaction of hostility to insignificant irritants.
Consistent pattern of challenging or disrespectful treatment of authority figures.
Use of verbally abusive language.

Goals: Decrease overall intensity and frequency of angry feelings in provocative situations.
Learn effective coping behaviors to stop escalation and resolve conflicts.
Express anger in a controlled, respectful manner with reasonable judgment regarding time and place.

Objectives

1. Verbalize an understanding of the two-step model of anger.

2. Implement the combined use of deep muscle relaxation, safe place visualization, and slow abdominal breathing.

Interventions

1. Teach that anger is a two-step process, requiring both (1) experience of pain (physical or emotional) and packaging. (2) use of trigger thoughts (attributions that blame others for the painful experience) to discharge arousal.

2. Facilitate group discussion about anger's self-perpetuating cycle of anger: anger–trigger thoughts–more anger. Encourage members to share their own experiences with this cycle.

1. Lead group members through entire combined relaxation program: progressive muscle relaxation (without tension), followed by safe place visualization, and finally deep abdominal breathing using cue words.

2. Assign members to practice the entire sequence daily during the week and report on their progress the following week.

(Continued)

3. Identify own common trigger thoughts for anger.	1. Give group members a list describing major trigger thoughts, including three types of shoulds: *entitlement* ("I want it so much, I should be able to have it"); *fairness* ("It's fair, so it should happen"); and *change* ("If I persist enough, she should do it my way"); and three types of blamers: *assumed intent* ("He's doing that deliberately to upset me"); *magnification* ("This is so awful, she's always doing it"); and *global labeling* ("He's so lazy [stupid, selfish, etc.]").
	2. Elicit from group members personal examples of the use of each type of trigger thought and the resulting anger.
	3. Facilitate the development of a list of coping self-talk for each category of trigger thoughts and a list of general coping statements ("I can stay calm and relaxed," "Getting mad won't help"), and make copies for each group member.
4. Use imagery to practice coping skills in medium-anger situations.	1. Assign group members to identify two midrange anger scenes (5 or 6 on scale of 10).
	2. Lead members through several imagery coping skills rehearsals of midrange anger scenes.
5. Use imagery to practice coping skills in high-anger situations.	1. Assign group members to identify two high-range anger scenes (9 or 10 on scale of 10).
	2. Lead group members through several coping skills rehearsals using high-anger scenes (9 or 10 on scale of 10); stay in the

(Continued)

scenes using relaxation and positive self-statements to reduce anger arousal.

Group Member Diagnosis: 312.34   Intermittent Explosive Disorder

ADULT CHILDREN OF ALCOHOLICS

BEHAVIORAL DEFINITIONS

1. A history of being raised in an alcoholic home that resulted in having experienced emotional abandonment, role confusion, abuse, and a chaotic, unpredictable environment.
2. Inability to trust others, share feelings, or talk openly about self.
3. Overly concerned with the welfare of other people.
4. Passive-submissive to the wishes, wants, and needs of others; too eager to please others.
5. Chronically fearful of interpersonal abandonment and desperately clings to destructive relationships.
6. Tells other people what they want to hear rather than the truth.
7. Persistent feelings of worthlessness and a belief that being treated with disdain is normal and expected.
8. Strong feelings of panic and helplessness when faced with being alone as a close relationship ends.
9. Chooses partners and friends who are chemically dependent or have other serious problems.
10. Distrusts authority figures—trusts only peers.
11. Takes on the parental role in a relationship.
12. Chronic feelings of alienation from others.

—. _____

_____

—. _____

_____

—. _____

_____

LONG-TERM GOALS

1. Decrease dependence on relationships while beginning to meet own needs, build confidence, and practice assertiveness.
2. Demonstrate healthy communication that is honest, open, and self-disclosing.
3. Recognize adult child of an alcoholic traits and their detrimental effects on relationships.
4. Reduce the frequency of behaviors exclusively designed to please others.
5. Demonstrate the ability to recognize, accept, and meet the needs of self.
6. Replace negative, self-defeating thinking with self-enhancing messages to self.
7. Choose partners and friends who are responsible, respectful, and reliable.
8. Overcome fears of abandonment, loss, and neglect as the source of these feelings (i.e., being raised in an alcoholic home) becomes clear.
9. Reduce feelings of alienation and improve feelings of self-worth.

__. _____
   _____

__. _____
   _____

__. _____
   _____

SHORT-TERM OBJECTIVES

1. Verbalize problems related to being an adult child of an alcoholic (ACOA) that have led to participating in the group. (1)

2. Verbalize an understanding of ACOA characteristics and their negative impact on life. (2, 3)

3. Describe own ACOA traits as experienced in daily interactions. (4)

THERAPEUTIC INTERVENTIONS

1. Ask each group member to describe life problems that precipitated joining the group.

2. Elicit group members' understanding of traits characteristic of adult children of alcoholics (ACOA).

3. Present additional material of ACOA traits if necessary to supplement members' knowledge, and teach an ac-

4. List childhood family experiences that shape behavior, thoughts, and emotions into an ACOA pattern. (5)

5. Verbalize feelings surrounding childhood family experiences of conflict. (6, 7, 8)

6. Identify own role within family of origin. (9, 10)

7. Describe how the role played in childhood family influences current relationships. (4, 11)

8. Verbalize an understanding of the rules of "don't talk, don't trust, don't feel" that were learned in family of origin and cite examples of how they were implemented in own experience. (12, 13)

9. List the negative impact on interpersonal relationships of the rules "don't talk, don't trust, don't feel." (4, 11, 13)

10. Identify own alcohol problem and follow through with a referral for treatment. (14)

11. Verbalize the difference between emotional needs and personal desires. (15)

12. Identify own emotional needs and personal desires. (16)

13. Practice the expression of own emotional needs and personal desires within the group first and then in daily life circumstances. (17, 18, 19)

14. Ask someone outside the group for help in meeting

curate understanding of this pattern of behavior. Assign reading of *It Will Never Happen to Me* (Black) or *Codependent No More* (Beattie).

4. Elicit from group members examples of their own behavior that corresponds to the typical ACOA characteristics.

5. Teach group members how the lack of consistency, predictability, and safety, the secrecy and fear, combine to result in ACOA traits, soliciting from members examples of experiences that shaped their personality.

6. Describe the family-sculpting exercise.

7. Have each member sculpt a typical scene of turmoil in his or her family, using other group members as role players. The active member positions each person, explains who he or she represents in the family, and directs the verbal and physical interaction.

8. After each sculpting exercise, process the group members' feelings arising from directing, role-playing, or witnessing the experience.

9. Teach group members the four potential roles adopted by children of alcoholics as described in *It Will Never Happen to Me* (Black): the

own emotional needs and personal desires. (18, 19)

15. Identify fears of not being in control of situations. (20, 21)

16. Verbalize the link between growing up in an alcoholic family and the need to control. (22)

17. Identify own attempts at controlling others' behaviors. (23)

18. Describe what can reasonably be expected to be controlled and what situations cannot be controlled. (23, 24)

19. Verbalize an understanding of the concept of a higher power and how a spiritual faith in this higher power can reduce the need to be in control. (25)

20. Verbalize an understanding of the concept of compassionate detachment versus rejection. (26, 27)

21. Report on the *in vivo* practice of compassionate detachment toward others' needs in order to reduce caretaking behavior. (28, 29, 30)

22. Verbalize an understanding of where own responsibility for satisfying others' emotional needs begins and ends. (31, 32)

23. Identify own feelings, and express them openly and assertively in group. (33, 34, 35, 36, 37)

responsible one, the adjuster, the placater, and the acting-out child.

10. Facilitate group discussion of the four roles adopted by children of alcoholics and help members identify their own role within their family of origin.

11. Encourage group sharing of how own role within family of origin affects current interpersonal relationships.

12. Teach group members about the unspoken rule in alcoholic families that the alcoholism remain a secret (*don't talk*), about the chaos that requires children to rely only on themselves (*don't trust*), and about the denial of feelings that results from such a situation (*don't feel*). See *It Will Never Happen to Me* (Black).

13. Facilitate group discussion about the *don't talk, don't trust, don't feel* rules that were learned in the family of origin, highlighting the negative impact of these rules on all interpersonal relationships.

14. Evaluate each member's current alcohol and substance use and make an appropriate referral where necessary.

15. Clarify the differences between emotional needs (e.g., to be loved, to be accepted) and personal desires (e.g., to go to the movies, to get a

24. Identify fears of expressing anger, including the fear of being abandoned. (38, 39)

25. Communicate feelings openly and honestly with significant others outside the group. (40, 41)

26. Demonstrate congruity between thoughts/feelings and verbal and nonverbal communication. (42, 43)

27. Identify and implement self-nurturing behaviors. (44)

28. Identify negative, distorted cognitions that maintain ACOA behaviors. (45)

29. Replace distorted cognitions with reality-based, self-affirming cognitions. (46, 47, 48)

30. Report a reduction in feelings of shame, worthlessness, fear, and alienation. (37, 46, 47, 48)

31. Verbalize an understanding of the elements of trust. (49)

32. Participate in a "trust walk." (50)

—. _____
   _____
—. _____
   _____
—. _____
   _____

new job, to eat Thai food for dinner).

16. Assist group members in identifying their emotional needs and personal desires.

17. Use role playing and modeling to teach assertiveness, and then have group members practice assertive requests in small groups.

18. Assign group members to express emotional needs and personal desires during the week, including asking for help or support.

19. Process the group members' success in attempting to assertively express their needs and desires.

20. Explore members' feelings about the situations in which they do not have control.

21. Encourage group sharing of members' fears of giving up attempts to be in control.

22. Facilitate group discussion about the link between the chaos and unpredictability of growing up in an alcoholic home and the current need to be in control.

23. Encourage group exploration of ways in which members attempt to control others' behavior.

24. Elicit examples from group members of situations over which they have control versus situations over which they do not have control.

25. Encourage group discussion of the concept of a higher power that runs the universe and how acceptance of this concept helps with letting go of control and turning concerns over to the higher power. Encourage members to share their own ideas (or alternative) of this concept.

26. Teach group members the relationship between letting go of control and the concept of compassionate detachment (i.e., caring for another person but maintaining boundaries of responsibility for behavior and decisions).

27. Have group members discuss the distinction between detachment and rejection and relate it to their own lives.

28. In small groups, have members develop strategies for handling situations at home with detachment (i.e., maintaining boundaries of responsibility).

29. Assign group members to try using at least one of their detachment strategies with significant others during the week.

30. Review members' experiences in applying detachment strategies during the week, reinforcing successes and further strategizing for failures.

31. Teach group members the differences between enmeshed relationships and those with healthy boundaries.

32. Have group members sculpt examples of enmeshed relationships and those with healthy boundaries.

33. Assist group members in identifying own feelings (i.e., using "I" statements: "I feel _____ when you _____ because _____"; "I would like _____") as they pertain to material raised in the group.

34. Teach active listening skills (e.g., listen with full attention, listen for the feelings, ask clarifying questions, acknowledge by paraphrasing) as an alternative to solution-finding responses; confront any inappropriate ownership of responsibility.

35. Reinforce the appropriate expression of feelings in the group.

36. Facilitate group discussion of the idea that the honest, open expression of feelings is a healthy alternative to controlling, ACOA behavior.

37. Teach group members how expressing feelings and needs honestly and openly is most critical when situations stir up feelings of shame, worthlessness, fear, and alienation.

38. Elicit group members' fears of expressing anger, including their fear of being abandoned by those they love if they express anger toward them.

39. Encourage group members to write out their angry feelings before expressing them in "I" statements.

40. Facilitate the development of feeling statements for each group member about people they care about. Assign members to use at least one of their feeling statements during the week.

41. Review members' success using feeling statements with significant others.

42. Elicit group members' examples of own behavior that was congruent with their feelings and thoughts, as well as examples of incongruent behavior.

43. Demonstrate and encourage group members to provide empathic confrontation of incongruity in any members' behavior.

44. Facilitate group brainstorming of self-nurturing behavior (e.g., taking a walk, listening to music, taking a bath), and assign members to practice at least one self-nurturing behavior each day.

45. Assist group members in identifying negative, distorted cognitions that fuel and maintain ACOA behaviors.

46. Teach group members thought-stopping techniques (e.g., mentally shouting "Stop," snapping a rubber band around the wrist), and encourage them to practice *in vivo*.

47. Teach group members how to challenge the negative, distorted cognitions using Socratic questioning.

48. Facilitate the development of reality-based, self-affirming cognitions to replace the distorted cognitions, and demonstrate the link between positive, realistic thoughts and calm feelings of self-esteem.

49. Encourage group discussion of the characteristics that are necessary for building trust between two people (honesty, self-disclosure, acceptance, etc.).

50. Assign pairs of group members to go on a "trust walk," where one member leads another "blind" member (eyes closed or blindfolded) on a walk around the room. Each sighted leader helps the "blind" person explore the surroundings using touch, sound, and smell. Process the blind members'

difficulty in letting go of
control and trusting the
partner.

—. _____

_____

—. _____

_____

—. _____

_____

DIAGNOSTIC SUGGESTIONS

Axis I: 311   Depressive Disorder NOS
              300.00   Anxiety Disorder NOS
              309.81   Posttraumatic Stress Disorder
              300.4   Dysthymic Disorder

              _____   _____

              _____   _____

Axis II: 301.82   Avoidant Personality Disorder
              301.6   Dependent Personality Disorder
              301.9   Personality Disorder NOS

              _____   _____

              _____   _____

AGORAPHOBIA/PANIC

BEHAVIORAL DEFINITIONS

1. Unexpected, sudden, and repeated panic symptoms (shallow breathing, sweating, heart racing or pounding, dizziness, depersonalization or derealization, trembling, chest tightness, fear of dying or losing control, nausea).
2. Fear of having another panic attack in situations where escape is perceived to be difficult.
3. Avoidance of those situations where panic attacks have previously occurred or where they may occur.
4. Dependence on the company of a support person, including spouse or partner, on ventures outside the home.
5. Mild depression in the face of a decreasing range of possible activities.
6. Prevalence of negative, anxiety-producing self-talk.
7. Sensitivity to environmental stimuli (temperature, light, sounds, smells).
8. Sensitivity to other people and their feelings.
9. Tendency to please others over own needs and desires.
10. Very rich and vivid imagination.
11. High degree of emotional reactivity.
12. Tendency toward perfectionism.

—. _____

_____

—. _____

_____

—. _____

_____

LONG-TERM GOALS

1. Reduce incidence of panic attacks.
2. Reduce fear so that he/she can independently and freely leave home and comfortably be in public environments.
3. Reduce panic symptoms and the fear that they will recur without the ability to cope with and control them.
4. Replace anxiety-provoking cognitions with reality-based, self-affirming cognitions.
5. Increase feelings of self-esteem while reducing feelings of inadequacy, insecurity, and shame.
6. Reduce experience of general social anxiety.

—. _____

_____

—. _____

_____

—. _____

_____

SHORT-TERM OBJECTIVES

1. Get to know another person in a social context. (1)
2. Verbalize an understanding and acceptance of the ground rules of the group. (2, 3)
3. Agree to do homework consistently. (2, 3)
4. Describe the history of panic attacks. (4)
5. Verbalize an understanding of the development of agoraphobia and relate it to own experience. (5)
6. Identify a safe person (or place) on which dependence exists. (6)

THERAPEUTIC INTERVENTIONS

1. Have members introduce each other in dyads (paired with a stranger) and then introduce their partner to the group.
2. Explain and discuss the ground rules, including necessity of doing homework, asking permission to leave the room to calm down if feeling anxious (and returning if at all possible), sharing weekly progress without discussing specific anxiety symptoms, and avoiding unnecessary anxiety-provoking situations until

7. Verbalize an understanding of how depression often stems from the shrinking from daily opportunities for activity. (7)

8. Identify within self the characteristic personality traits of the agoraphobic person. (8)

9. Give support to and accept support from other group members. (9)

10. Verbalize an understanding of the long-term, predisposing factors that lead to agoraphobia and relate them to own experience. (10, 11)

11. Identify own level of cumulative stress and its relationship to a vulnerability to panic attacks. (12, 13)

12. Describe first panic attack and its triggering event or situation. (14)

13. Identify those elements that maintain own agoraphobia. (15)

14. Practice abdominal breathing and progressive relaxation to reduce stress level. (16, 17, 19)

15. Implement visualization of a peaceful scene to reduce stress. (18, 19)

16. Exercise aerobically at least four times per week for at least 20 to 30 minutes. (20, 21)

17. Verbalize an understanding of the panic cycle. (22)

appropriate skills have been learned.

3. Teach group members that fears must be addressed on a daily basis in order for recovery to proceed and that relaxation, exercise, desensitization, and cognitive restructuring must be practiced consistently to achieve this.

4. Elicit from group members their history of panic attacks, including circumstantial triggers, severity, symptom pattern, chronicity, and attempts at coping or resolution.

5. Teach group members how agoraphobia can develop as a complication in a person suffering from panic attacks if one develops a pattern of avoidance, not just of the situation in which the attack occurred, but of the possibility of another panic attack in any remotely similar situation.

6. Facilitate group discussion of the dependence on a safe person and/or safe place that resulted from (or contributed to) their agoraphobia.

7. Explore with group members the hopelessness and helplessness they experience as a result of their avoidance.

8. Assist group members in identifying within themselves the characteristic

18. Verbalize an accurate understanding of the nature of panic attacks. (23)

19. Report success at accepting, observing, and floating with the feelings of panic when they occur rather than fighting them. (24, 25)

20. Articulate the distinction between first and second fear. (26)

21. Use coping statements to facilitate an attitude of calm acceptance toward panic attacks and to float with the waves of panic. (27)

22. Use personal anxiety scale to identify early stages of panic. (28, 29)

23. Temporarily withdraw from a situation when anxiety of level 4 is reached and return to it when anxiety is reduced. (30, 31, 32)

24. Report success in using diversion techniques to reduce panic. (33, 34)

25. Report success using abdominal breathing. (16, 17, 35)

26. Report success using coping statements along with relaxation skills to reduce panic. (16, 17, 27, 36)

27. Keep a journal of panic attack symptoms, environmental circumstance, severity rating, and coping strategies used. (37, 38)

28. Make appropriate decision regarding the need for med-

personality traits of the agoraphobic person (e.g., sensitivity to environmental stimuli, sensitivity to other people's feelings and needs, a "people pleaser," creative and intelligent, rich and vivid imagination, high emotional reactivity, prevalence of negative thinking, tendency toward perfectionism, tendency to avoid by procrastination, shame and secrecy about the problem).

9. Foster group cohesiveness by distributing, after permission has been privately obtained, a list of the names and phone numbers of all members. Ask each member to call one other (different) member each week to talk for at least a few minutes to get further acquainted or to share a success achieved during the week.

10. Teach group members the predisposing causes of agoraphobia that occur in childhood, which can include parents who communicate an overly cautious view of the world, are overly critical, set excessively high standards, or are emotionally abusive, as well as traumatic experiences that lead to tremendous insecurity. Stress to members that agoraphobic responses are learned and therefore can be unlearned, regardless of predisposition.

ication to reduce panic symptoms. (39)

29. Verbalize an understanding of the concepts of sensitization and desensitization. (40)

30. Complete successful desensitization protocol using imagery. (41, 42, 43, 44)

31. Confront own resistance to undertaking exposure to a fear-inducing situation or tolerating anxiety in those situations. (45)

32. Verbalize an understanding of difference between avoidance and temporary retreat. (45)

33. Complete successful *in vivo* desensitization. (46, 47)

34. Reward self for small successes that demonstrate any progress at all. (48)

35. Identify negative, anxiety-provoking cognitions. (49)

36. Develop reality-based, self-affirming cognitions to challenge and replace the negative, anxiety-provoking cognitions. (50, 51, 52)

37. Identify the mistaken beliefs that fuel the anxiety-provoking cognitions, and counter with positive affirmations. (53, 54, 55)

38. Express feelings, including anger, openly and honestly in group and then with significant others. (56, 57)

39. Verbalize the difference between behaviors that are

11. Have group members share those predisposing factors that pertain to their own experiences.

12. Facilitate group discussion of the way stress accumulates when it is not dealt with and how it can lead to psychophysiological illnesses, including panic attacks. Encourage members to identify their cumulative levels of stress.

13. Assign group members to fill out a Holmes and Rahe stress chart to identify recent stressors that could be contributing to their agoraphobia.

14. Elicit from group members the stories of their first panic attack and the situations that triggered them.

15. Describe the factors that contribute to the maintenance of agoraphobia (e.g., phobic avoidance; self-talk that fosters anxiety; inability to assertively express feelings, needs, and wants; inadequate self-nurturing skills; a high-stress lifestyle; and a lack of meaning or purpose in life). Encourage group members to identify those factors with which they identify.

16. Teach deep-breathing technique, instructing group members to inhale slowly and deeply, pause, and exhale slowly and completely.

passive, aggressive, and assertive, and then demonstrate assertive expression of feelings in group and with significant others. (58, 59)

40. Increase the implementation of self-nurturing behaviors. (60, 61, 62)

41. Decrease consumption of caffeine and refined sugar and focus on good nutrition. (63)

42. Verbalize a commitment to relapse-prevention program. (64)

—. _____
   _____

—. _____
   _____

—. _____
   _____

17. Lead members through progressive relaxation protocol, where each muscle group is first tightened and then relaxed. Stress the need for daily practice.

18. Guide members through a visualization of a peaceful scene, eliciting as many details of the scene as possible. Encourage members to practice visualization daily after relaxation protocol.

19. Review members' success using progressive relaxation and visualization during the week.

20. Describe to group members the anxiety-reducing effects of aerobic exercise, and elicit a commitment from each member to incorporate exercise into their daily routine at least four times a week for at least 20 to 30 minutes. Recommend reading _Exercising Your Way to Better Mental Health_ (Leith.)

21. Have members report back to the group on their progress in meeting their exercise commitment.

22. Teach the concept of the panic cycle, where a physical or emotional trigger leads to body symptoms of panic (heart palpitations, shortness of breath, sweating, dizziness, trembling, tightness in the chest, etc.). The negative thoughts that immediately follow the be-

ginning of body symptoms lead to intensified body symptoms, which in turn lead to more negative, catastrophic thoughts and result finally in a full-blown panic attack. Elicit group members' experiences that conform to the panic cycle.

23. Present accurate information (e.g., that panic attacks are simply the fight-or-flight response occurring out of context; that they are not dangerous and will not result in heart attack, fainting, dizziness, or going crazy) that counters the myths regarding the nature of panic attacks.

24. Introduce the concept of accepting and observing rather than fighting the panic attack. Discuss floating with the "wave" of panic, and explain that the physiological concomitants of the fight-or-flight response are time-limited and will end of their own accord.

25. Assign group members to practice observing the pattern of their panic attacks and to try floating with the panic rather than fighting it. Have members report back to the group on their success.

26. Describe to the group the distinction between the first fear (i.e., the actual physiological reactions underlying panic) and second fear (i.e.,

the one elicited by the negative, frightening self-statements made in response to first fear).

27. Provide group members with a list of coping statements (e.g., "I can be anxious and still deal with this situation"; "This is just anxiety, it won't kill me"; "I've survived this before and I'll survive it now") to encourage acceptance and a willingness to float with the panic rather than fighting it.

28. Help group members develop a personal anxiety scale from 0 (calm and relaxed) to 10 (terror, major panic attack), using 4 (marked anxiety) as the point between tolerable anxiety and out-of-control panic. Have members identify specific personal physiological signs that indicate a potential panic attack.

29. Ask group members to use personal anxiety scale to identify early stages of panic (4 or below), when intervention is still possible.

30. Explain to group members the concept of being sensitized to a situation by staying in it while experiencing increased anxiety. Describe how a phobia to that situation could be developed or, if already in existence, reinforced.

31. Teach group members the strategy of withdrawing temporarily from situations where anxiety level of 4 is reached, and then returning after anxiety is reduced.

32. Ask group members to use the withdrawal strategy during the week, and then have them report back to the group on their success.

33. Assign the practice of diversion strategies (talking to someone; engaging in physical activity; doing something that requires intense concentration; practicing thought-stopping techniques, etc.) to help abort a panic attack before anxiety reaches levels higher than 4.

34. Review members' use of diversion strategies, reinforcing successes and redirecting failures.

35. Assign group members to use abdominal breathing and relaxation during the week to abort panic attacks in which anxiety levels are at 4 or below. Have members report back to the group on their success.

36. Assign group members to choose three or four coping statements and practice them with abdominal breathing and relaxation, first in group and then *in vivo* during the week.

37. Have group members keep a log of their panic attacks

during the week, noting when and where the attack occurred, what triggers might have precipitated the attack, the maximum intensity of the attack based on their personal anxiety scale, and the coping strategies they used to abort or limit the attack.

38. Have members share with the group insights gained from the log.

39. Help group members evaluate their need for medication in handling severe attacks, and make appropriate referrals to a physician.

40. Teach group members the concepts of sensitization and desensitization using both imagery and *in vivo* experiences.

41. Help group members construct an appropriate desensitization hierarchy for a phobic situation, from least to most anxiety-provoking stimuli. Encourage members to include reality-based details of each step of the hierarchy.

42. Lead group members through the steps of systematic desensitization, repeating the scene until it no longer has the capacity to raise anxiety levels above level 1 on the personal anxiety scale before progressing to the next scene in hierarchy.

43. Assign group members to continue working on desensitization protocol every day for 20 minutes. Ask members to develop hierarchies for three other phobic situations.

44. Review members' success in working on desensitization hierarchies.

45. Facilitate group discussion of possible resistance to the discomfort and hard work of *in vivo* desensitization, emphasizing the difference between avoidance and temporary retreat. Teach that sometimes anxiety gets worse before it gets better.

46. Assign group members to begin *in vivo* desensitization with their safe person. Stress the exposure-retreat-recover-return cycle that is a part of systematic desensitization *in vivo*.

47. Review members' success with *in vivo* desensitization.

48. Help group members develop a reward system for reinforcing small steps toward recovery.

49. Clarify distinction between thoughts and feelings. Help group members identify the distorted, negative thoughts that trigger fear and anxiety.

50. Help members develop (using the Socratic method of questioning), reality-based, self-affirming cogni-

tions to challenge and replace anxiety-provoking cognitions.

51. Assign group members to practice *in vivo* challenging and replacing their negative, anxiety-provoking cognitions with realistic, self-affirming thoughts.

52. Review members' experience with cognitive restructuring, reinforcing success and redirecting failure.

53. Explore with group members the underlying mistaken beliefs that fuel anxiety-provoking cognitions (e.g., "People won't like me if they see who I really am"; "I don't deserve to be happy and successful"; "It's terrible to fail"; "I should (never) be _____").

54. Challenge members' beliefs using the Socratic method of questioning, and help them develop affirmations to counter the mistaken beliefs.

55. Assign group members to use their affirmations during the week to challenge mistaken beliefs, and report on their success.

56. Explore with group members their fears about expressing anger, including fears of losing control or of alienating their safe person.

57. Help members write out their angry feelings before communicating them to another person.

58. Clarify the distinction between passive, aggressive, and assertive behaviors. Then role-play situations where members make assertive requests of their dyad partners.

59. Encourage honest, assertive expression of feelings within the group and then with significant others.

60. Introduce the concept of the inner child who carries the pain of childhood trauma.

61. Help members develop a list of self-nurturing behaviors to heal feelings of neglect or abuse, and assign daily completion of at least one item from the list.

62. Have members report to the group their success in self-nurturing.

63. Explore with group members their use of caffeine and refined sugar and the influence of these chemicals on anxiety and depression via hypoglycemia. Discuss the importance of decreasing the use of both, as well as focusing on good nutrition and vitamin/mineral balance to increase stress resistance.

64. Elicit commitment from group members to a relapse-prevention program consisting of daily relaxation, physical exercise, good nutrition, and cognitive restructuring. Include

twice-weekly sessions of imagery and *in vivo* desensitization around specific fears.

—.   _____
     _____

—.   _____
     _____

—.   _____
     _____

DIAGNOSTIC SUGGESTIONS

Axis I: 300.21   Panic Disorder With Agoraphobia
                300.22   Agoraphobia Without History of Panic
                            Disorder
                300.01   Panic Disorder Without Agorophobia
                _____   _____
                _____   _____

Axis II: 301.6   Dependent Personality Disorder
                _____   _____
                _____   _____

ANGER CONTROL PROBLEMS

BEHAVIORAL DEFINITIONS

1. Overreaction of hostility to insignificant irritants.
2. Swift and harsh judgments made to or about others.
3. Body language of tense muscles (e.g., clenched fist or jaw, glaring looks, or refusal to make eye contact).
4. Use of passive-aggressive patterns (social withdrawal due to anger, lack of complete or timely compliance in following directions or rules, complaining about authority figures behind their backs, or refusal to meet expected behavioral norms).
5. Consistent pattern of challenging or disrespectful treatment of authority figures.
6. Use of verbally abusive language.
7. Recognition and admission of negative consequences of poor anger control (in terms of relationships, health, work life, etc.).
8. No history of physical violence against either persons or property.
9. No current abuse of drugs or alcohol.

—. _____

_____

—. _____

_____

—. _____

_____

LONG-TERM GOALS

1. Decrease overall intensity and frequency of angry feelings in provocative situations.

2. Learn effective coping behaviors to stop escalation and resolve conflicts.
3. Express anger in a controlled, respectful manner with reasonable judgment regarding time and place.

—. _____

_____

—. _____

_____

—. _____

_____

SHORT-TERM OBJECTIVES

1. State reason for participating in group. (1)
2. Verbalize an understanding of goals and ground rules of the group therapy experience. (2)
3. Keep a log of circumstances surrounding the experience of anger. (3, 4)
4. Verbalize an understanding of the two-step model of anger. (5, 6)
5. Verbalize an awareness of the futility of ventilation as an anger-control tool. (7)
6. Verbalize the distinction between anger and aggressive behavior. (8, 9)
7. Articulate a commitment to coping with pain rather than blaming with anger. (10)
8. Demonstrate mastery of progressive muscle relax-

THERAPEUTIC INTERVENTIONS

1. Ask members to introduce themselves to the rest of the group and explain why they are seeking help.
2. Clarify goals of the group therapy experience and ground rules, emphasizing importance of homework.
3. Assign group members to keep anger log to facilitate self-observation. Entries include date, time, the situation, anger-triggering thoughts, emotional arousal (on a 1 to 10 scale), and aggressive behavior (on a 1 to 10 scale).
4. Review members' anger logs and have members share with the group insights gained.
5. Teach that anger is a two-step process, requiring both (1) experience of pain (physical or emotional) and (2)

ation and relaxation without tension. (11, 12, 13, 14)

9. Demonstrate mastery of visualization of a safe place.
(15, 17, 18)

10. Demonstrate quick reflexive
use of safe place visualization in group and *in vivo*
stressful situations. (16)

11. Demonstrate use of cue
word coupled with deep, abdominal breathing. (19, 20)

12. Implement the combined
use of deep-muscle relax-
ation, safe place visualization, and slow abdominal
breathing. (21, 22)

13. Verbalize an understanding
of Ellis's ABC model of explaining how thoughts lead
to emotion. (23, 24)

14. Verbalize an increased
awareness of trigger
thoughts that generate
anger. (25)

15. Identify own common trigger thoughts for anger. (26)

16. List coping self-talk statements for use in response to
trigger thoughts. (27)

17. Demonstrate use in imagery of the coping skills of
relaxation and positive self-
talk in low-anger situations.
(28, 29, 30)

18. Monitor effects of relaxation
and coping self-talk in
anger log. (31, 32)

19. Use imagery to practice
coping skills in medium-
anger situations.
(33, 34, 35, 36, 37, 38)

use of trigger thoughts (attributions that blame
others for the painful experience) to discharge arousal.

6. Facilitate group discussion
about anger's self-
perpetuating cycle of anger:
anger–trigger
thoughts–more anger. En-
courage members to share
their own experiences with
this cycle.

7. Elicit group members' beliefs about the value of
venting anger; then correct
misperceptions by teaching
that ventilation increases
rather than dissipates
anger.

8. Clarify the distinction between anger as an emotion
and aggression as a behavior. Emphasize that they
can occur independently.

9. Elicit examples from group
members of the indepen-
dent occurrence of anger
and aggressive behavior.

10. Encourage group discussion
about the choice between
developing coping strategies
to deal with the painful experience versus blaming
others for the pain, emphasizing the advantages of the
former alternative.

11. Teach progressive muscle
relaxation, tensing and then
relaxing each muscle group
in the body.

12. Teach muscle relaxation of
each muscle group without

20. Use imagery to practice coping skills in high-anger situations. (30, 40, 41)

21. Verbalize an understanding of active and passive Response Choice Rehearsal (RCR). (42, 43)

22. Demonstrate memorization of six RCR responses. (44)

23. Verbalize own need statements, negotiating statements, and self-care solutions assertively, not aggressively. (45, 51)

24. Verbalize an understanding of the ways in which RCR responses can be used. (46, 47)

25. Demonstrate flexible use of the six RCR responses in role-play situations. (48, 49, 50, 51)

26. Report success on leaving anger-arousing situations if withdrawal statement is ignored. (52)

27. Demonstrate flexible use *in vivo* of the six RCR responses in low-, medium-, and high-anger situations. (53, 54, 55)

—. _____

   _____

—. _____

   _____

—. _____

   _____

using intentional muscle tension.

13. Assign members to practice progressive muscle relaxation daily, with and without using intentional muscle tension.

14. Have members report back to the group on their success in using progressive muscle relaxation.

15. Lead group members in a detailed visualization of a personal "safe place" where they feel relaxed and safe.

16. Have members practice visualizing their safe place quickly, then returning to the group. Tell them to stay one minute in each place, cycling back and forth to achieve reflexive use of this technique in stressful situations.

17. Assign members to practice safe place visualization daily after progressive muscle relaxation, as well as in any situation that has potential to provoke or disturb.

18. Review members' success in avoiding provocation using safe place visualization.

19. Teach group members deep, abdominal breathing, helping members push out their bellies with each breath.

20. Have group members select a cue word (e.g., *relax, peace, blue*) to use with deep abdominal breathing to cue relaxation. Instruct mem-

bers to say cue word on each exhalation.

21. Lead group members through entire combined relaxation program: progressive muscle relaxation (without tension), followed by safe place visualization, and finally deep abdominal breathing using cue words.

22. Assign members to practice the entire sequence daily during the week, and report on their progress the following week.

23. Teach Ellis's ABC model of emotion: A = activating event; B = belief (thought, interpretation, assumption); and C = consequence (emotion).

24. Encourage sharing of personal examples that fit the ABC model.

25. Give group members a list describing major trigger thoughts, including three types of shoulds: *entitlement* ("I want it so much, I should be able to have it"); *fairness* ("It's fair so it should happen"); and *change* ("If I insist enough, she should do it my way"); and three types of blamers: *assumed intent* ("He's doing that deliberately to upset me"); *magnification* ("This is so awful, she's always doing it"); and *global labeling* ("He's so lazy [stupid, selfish, etc."]).

26. Elicit from group members personal examples of the

use of each type of trigger thought and the resulting anger.

27. Facilitate development of a list of coping self-talk statements for each category of trigger thought and a list of general coping statements ("I can stay calm and relaxed," "Getting mad won't help"), and make copies for each group member.

28. Ask group members to select responses from each list that seem most useful to them.

29. Facilitate group discussion about coping statements that work the best. Help members who have problems generating effective coping statements.

30. Lead group members through several rehearsals in imagery of coping skills used with low-anger situations: (1) induce relaxation (progressive relaxation, visualization, breathing, and cue-controlled relaxation); (2) visualize in detail a low-anger scene (3 or 4 on a scale of 10) and use trigger thoughts to arouse anger; (3) erase scene, using relaxation skills and coping self-talk statements to become relaxed again.

31. Assign group members to include coping efforts in anger log, and note if emotional arousal or aggressive behavior decreases as a result.

32. Review members' progress in using positive self-talk and relaxation as indicated in anger logs, noting changes in frequency, intensity or duration of anger.

33. Assign group members to identify two midrange anger scenes (5 or 6 on scale of 10).

34. Lead members through several imagery coping skills rehearsals of midrange-anger scenes.

35. Have members share with the rest of the group their experiences with coping-skills rehearsal and effective coping self-statements.

36. Focus on particular trigger words and thoughts that members report difficulty coping with, and facilitate development of appropriate responses.

37. Lead group members through several coping-skills rehearsals of medium-anger (7 or 8 on scale of 10) scenes. Have members stay in the scene and practice relaxation and coping self-talk statements.

38. Encourage members to share their successes with the rest of the group in coping with high- to midrange-anger scenes.

39. Assign group members to identify two high-anger scenes (9 or 10 on scale of 10).

40. Lead group members through several coping-skills rehearsals using high-anger scenes (9 or 10 on scale of 10), staying in the scenes using relaxation and positive self-statements to reduce anger arousal.

41. Celebrate with members their successes in coping with high-anger scenes.

42. Teach three *active* (when client is feeling anger) Response Choice Rehearsal (RCR) opening statements (McKay and Rogers): (1) Ask for what you need/want ("I'm feeling _____, and what I think I need/want in this situation is _____"). (2) Negotiate ("What would you propose to solve this problem?"). (3) Use self-care ("If this continues, I'll have to _____ in order to take care of myself").

43. Teach three *passive* (when other person is feeling anger) RCR opening statements (McKay and Rogers): (1) Get information ("What do you need in this situation?" "What concerns you?" What's bothering you in this situation?"). (2) Acknowledge ("So what you want is _____"; "So what concerns/bothers you is _____"). (3) Withdraw ("It feels like we're starting to get upset"; "I want to stop and cool off for awhile").

44. Emphasize the need for memorization of statements for the benefits of de-escalation to accrue. Assign group members to memorize RCR opening statements.

45. Help group members develop appropriate, assertive need/want statements, negotiating statements, and self-care solutions. Emphasize positive voice control (no sarcasm or anger).

46. Teach group members how to start with one RCR statement and switch if anger continues or if met with resistance. Switching can continue until success is achieved.

47. Teach members to switch, if stuck, from active to passive responses or from passive to active.

48. Have triads of group members role-play low-, medium-, and high-anger scenes (with one person the provocateur, one practicing the RCR responses, and the third coaching).

49. Facilitate group discussion about role-play experiences.

50. Coach group members in developing appropriate negotiation and compromise statements to use in role plays.

51. Confront members' statements that focus on revenge rather than on negotiating or self-care.

52. Encourage group members to leave a situation if their withdrawal statement is ignored.

53. Assign members to practice *in vivo* RCR with a low-risk person with whom they've had conflict. Have them plan ahead their need/want statement, a fallback position, and a self-care solution.

54. Have members report back to the rest of the group their success with *in vivo* RCR situations.

55. Assign members to practice *in vivo* RCR in medium- and high-anger situations and report back to the group.

___. _____

_____

___. _____

_____

___. _____

_____

DIAGNOSTIC SUGGESTIONS

Axis I: 312.81   Conduct Disorder/Childhood Onset Type
312.82   Conduct Disorder/Adolescent Onset Type
296.xx   Bipolar I Disorder
312.34   Intermittent Explosive Disorder

_____   _____

_____   _____

Axis II: 301.83   Borderline Personality Disorder
301.7   Antisocial Personality Disorder

_____   _____

_____   _____

ANXIETY

BEHAVIORAL DEFINITIONS

1. Excessive daily anxiety and worry, without factual or logical basis, about several life circumstances.
2. Symptoms of motor tension, such as restlessness, tiredness, shakiness, or muscle tension.
3. Symptoms of autonomic hyperactivity, such as palpitations, shortness of breath, dizziness, dry mouth, trouble swallowing, nausea, or diarrhea.
4. Symptoms of hypervigilance, such as feeling constantly on edge, concentration difficulties, startling easily, trouble falling or staying asleep, and general state of irritability.
5. Prevalence of negative, anxiety-provoking self-talk.
6. A high degree of sensitivity to other people and their feelings.
7. Excessive tendency to please others over own needs and desires.
8. Tendency to perfectionism.

—. _____
   _____
—. _____
   _____
—. _____
   _____

LONG-TERM GOALS

1. Reduce overall level, frequency, and intensity of the anxiety so that daily functioning is not impaired.
2. Stabilize anxiety level while increasing ability to function on a daily basis.

3. Replace anxiety-provoking cognitions with reality-based, self-affirming cognitions.
4. Increase feelings of self-esteem while reducing feelings of inadequacy and insecurity regarding acceptance from others.

—. _____

_____

—. _____

_____

—. _____

_____

SHORT-TERM OBJECTIVES

1. Each member describe own anxiety symptoms that led to participating in anxiety group. (1)

2. Describe the history of feelings of anxiety and the impact on daily living. (2)

3. Verbalize an understanding of the long-term, predisposing causes of anxiety and relate them to own experience. (3, 4)

4. Identify own level of cumulative stress and its relationship to anxiety. (5, 6)

5. Identify the emotional, cognitive, and behavioral elements that maintain own anxiety. (7, 8)

6. Practice abdominal breathing and progressive muscle relaxation to reduce anxiety. (9)

7. Implement visualization of a peaceful scene to reduce stress. (10)

THERAPEUTIC INTERVENTIONS

1. Ask each member to describe his/her symptoms of anxiety and the incident that precipitated joining the anxiety group.

2. Have members describe their personal histories of anxiety, including the negative impact on their social and vocational functioning.

3. Teach group members the long-term, predisposing causes of anxiety (e.g., genetic predisposition; growing up in family where parents fostered overcautiousness, perfectionism, emotional insecurity, and dependence, or where parents suppressed assertiveness).

4. Have group members share the long-term, predisposing causes of anxiety that pertain to their own experiences.

8. Report on the degree of success in reducing anxiety when using abdominal breathing, progressive muscle relaxation, and visualization techniques. (11)

9. Exercise aerobically at least four times per week for at least 20 to 30 minutes. (12, 13, 14)

10. Identify own negative, anxiety-provoking self-talk. (15)

11. Verbalize the major types of cognitive distortions. (16)

12. Develop and implement reality-based, self-affirming cognitions to counter cognitive distortions and anxiety-provoking self-talk. (17, 18, 19)

13. Identify the mistaken beliefs that fuel anxiety-provoking cognitions. (20)

14. Report success in using positive affirmations to replace distorted, negative beliefs. (21, 22)

15. Report increased ability to identify and describe suppressed feelings. (23, 24, 25)

16. Express feelings, including anger, openly, honestly, and assertively in group and then with significant others. (26, 27, 28, 29)

17. Verbalize the difference between behaviors that are aggressive, passive, and assertive. (28)

5. Facilitate group discussion of the way stress accumulates when it is not dealt with and how it can lead to psychophysiological illnesses. Encourage members to identify their own cumulative levels of stress.

6. Assign group members to fill out a Holmes and Rahe stress chart to identify recent stressors that could be contributing to their anxiety.

7. Teach group members the emotional, cognitive, and behavioral elements that maintain anxiety (e.g., anxious self-talk, mistaken beliefs, withheld feelings, lack of assertiveness, muscle tension).

8. Encourage members to identify the elements that maintain their own anxiety.

9. Teach group members abdominal breathing and progressive muscle relaxation techniques.

10. Lead group members through detailed visualization of safe, peaceful place, and encourage daily use of this imagery following progressive muscle relaxation.

11. Assign members to practice abdominal breathing, progressive muscle relaxation, and safe place visualization daily and report back to group on their experience.

12. Describe to group members the physiological and psy-

18. Demonstrate assertive communication, including the expression of emotional needs and personal desires and the ability to say no. (29)

19. Demonstrate problem-solving skills. (30)

20. Demonstrate use of assertive techniques to avoid manipulation. (31, 32, 33)

21. Increase implementation of daily self nurturing behaviors. (34, 35)

22. Increase daily social involvement. (36)

23. Decrease consumption of caffeine and refined sugar and focus on good nutrition. (37)

24. Make appropriate decision regarding the need for medication to reduce anxiety. (38)

25. Verbalize a commitment to a relapse-prevention program. (39)

__. _____

_____

__. _____

_____

__. _____

_____

chological impact of exercise (e.g., rapid metabolism of excess adrenaline and thyroxin in the bloodstream; enhanced oxygenation of blood and brain, leading to improved concentration; production of endorphins; reduced insomnia; increased feelings of well-being; reduced depression).

13. Help group members formulate exercise programs building toward a goal of 20 to 30 minutes at least four days per week. Recommend *Exercising Your Way to Better Mental Health* (Leith).

14. Review members' experiences with their exercise programs, rewarding successes and supportively confronting resistance.

15. Clarify distinction between thoughts and feelings. Help group members identify the negative, anxiety-provoking thoughts that maintain their anxiety.

16. Teach group members the major types of cognitive distortions: *overestimating* ("If it was so awful this time, next time it could kill me"); *catastrophizing* ("If I don't follow through, I'll never be able to face my friends again"); *overgeneralizing* ("I always make bad judgments about potential employees"); *filtering* (responding to a single criticism in spite of a basically positive review) ("I

can't believe I messed up so badly"); *emotional reasoning* ("I feel overwhelmed, therefore I must not be competent to do the job"); *should statements* ("I should be able to do this without a single mistake"). Encourage members to share the distortions that trigger their own anxiety. Recommend *Ten Days to Self-Esteem* (Burns).

17. Help members, using the Socratic method of questioning, to develop reality-based, self-affirming cognitions to challenge and replace distorted, anxiety-provoking cognitions.

18. Assign group members to practice *in vivo* challenging and replacing their distorted, negative, anxiety-provoking cognitions with realistic, self-affirming ones.

19. Review members' experiences with cognitive restructuring, reinforcing success and redirecting strategies that fail.

20. Explore with group members the underlying mistaken beliefs that fuel anxiety-provoking cognitions (e.g., "People won't like me if they see who I really am"; "I don't deserve to be happy and successful"; "It's terrible to fail"; "I should (never) be _____").

21. Challenge members' distorted, negative beliefs re-

garding self by using the Socratic method of questioning, and help them develop self-affirmations to counter the mistaken beliefs.

22. Assign group members to use their self-affirmations during the week to challenge mistaken beliefs, and report on their success.

23. Help group members identify the symptoms of suppressed feelings that each experiences (e.g., free-floating anxiety, depression, psychosomatic symptoms such as headaches or ulcers, or muscle tension).

24. Give group members a handout listing a large number of feelings for use as personal reference in learning to label and talk about their feelings.

25. Teach group members steps to "tune in" to their bodies to identify their feelings (e.g., relax; pay attention to where in the body there are physical sensations; wait and listen to whatever arises; use the feelings list to clarify).

26. Explore with group members their fears about expressing anger, including fears of losing control or of alienating significant people.

27. Help members write out their angry feelings before communicating them to another person.

28. Clarify the distinction between passive, aggressive, and assertive behavior. Then role-play situations where members make assertive requests of their dyad partners.

29. Encourage honest, assertive expression of feelings in group and then with significant others.

30. Teach group members the five steps to assertive problem solving (i.e., identifying problem, brainstorming all possible options, evaluating each option, implementing course of action, and evaluating results), and role-play their application to everyday life conflicts.

31. Teach group members four techniques of responding to manipulation: *broken record technique* (repeating a request in calm, direct manner, such as "I would like to return this backpack and get a refund" to an uncooperative store clerk); *fogging* (agreeing to a possibly accurate part of a criticism, such as "You could be right that I'd look better if I made those changes"); *content-to-process shift* (changing the focus of discussion from the content to a description of what's going on between you, such as "You're making a joke, but it doesn't change my request"); *assertive inquiry* (used when an as-

sertive request is met with criticism, such as "Why is it a problem for you to let me leave on time today?").

32. Using the four assertiveness techniques to avoid manipulation, have small groups role-play life situations, and encourage members to implement the techniques during the week.

33. Review group members' experiences in responding to efforts to manipulate them, reinforcing successes and redirecting unsuccessful attempts.

34. Help members develop a list of self-nurturing behaviors (e.g., soak in a bath, read a book, listen to music), and assign daily completion of at least one item from the list.

35. Have members report to the group their success in self-nurturing.

36. Assign group members to participate in one social activity per day and report to the group on their experiences.

37. Explore with group members their use of caffeine and refined sugar and the influence of these chemicals on anxiety and depression via hypoglycemia. Discuss the importance of decreasing the use of both, as well as focusing on good nutrition and vitamin/mineral

balance to increase stress resistance.

38. Help group members evaluate their need for medication in handling their anxiety, and make appropriate referrals to a physician.

39. Elicit commitment from group members to a relapse-prevention program consisting of daily relaxation, physical exercise, good nutrition, and cognitive restructuring.

__. _____

_____

__. _____

_____

__. _____

_____

DIAGNOSTIC SUGGESTIONS

Axis I:	300.02	Generalized Anxiety Disorder
	300.00	Anxiety Disorder NOS
	309.24	Adjustment Disorder With Anxiety
	_____	_____
	_____	_____

ASSERTIVENESS DEFICIT

BEHAVIORAL DEFINITIONS

1. Difficulty in some situations expressing thoughts, feelings, and personal desires.
2. Fear of disapproval leads to reluctance to say no to requests for participation in an undesired activity.
3. Discomfort standing up for self in situations of conflict.
4. Passivity causes inability to seize opportunities.
5. Excessive tolerance of unpleasant situations.
6. Pattern of suppressing bad feelings until one single event triggers explosion of resentment.
7. Manifestations of stress-related physiological symptoms.
8. Social withdrawal.
9. Tendency to anticipate rejection or failure if assertive.
10. Presence of beliefs that limit rights to open expression of thoughts, feelings, and personal desires.

__. _____
   _____
__. _____
   _____
__. _____
   _____

LONG-TERM GOALS

1. Learn to differentiate and exhibit assertive communication from that which is passive and aggressive.
2. Modify beliefs that limit assertive expression of thoughts, feelings, and personal desires.

3. Demonstrate more assertive behavior in a wide range of situations.

—. _____

_____

—. _____

_____

—. _____

_____

SHORT-TERM OBJECTIVES

1. Describe examples of a lack of assertiveness from personal experience. (1)

2. Verbalize an awareness of own behavior in responding to different situations that call for assertive communication. (2)

3. Clarify distinction between assertive, passive, and aggressive communication, and give examples of each from own experience. (3, 4, 5)

4. Verbalize an increased awareness of nonverbal components of assertive communication. (6)

5. Identify the most significant problem areas for being assertive and set realistic goals for achieving assertiveness. (7, 8)

6. Verbalize an increased understanding of the basic premises underlying the different modes of communication. (9)

THERAPEUTIC INTERVENTIONS

1. Have members introduce themselves, giving examples of situations in which they were not assertive and would have liked to be.

2. Give group members handouts of problem situations and ask them to fill in how they would typically respond in each.

3. Teach the distinguishing characteristics of the three different modes of communicating: passive, aggressive, and assertive.

4. Elicit from group members examples of their own behavior that conforms to each of the different modes of communicating.

5. Use modeling to present examples of interactions where one person is communicating in either a passive, aggressive, or assertive manner. Ask group members to identify the particular mode of communicating in each interaction.

7. Identify mistaken traditional assumptions regarding social relationships. (10)

8. Verbalize assertive rights. (11, 12, 13, 14)

9. Identify fears related to consequences of being assertive. (15)

10. List and apply self-talk that challenges fears of being assertive. (16, 17, 18, 19)

11. Demonstrate use of the *broken-record* technique in group role plays. (20, 21, 22, 23)

12. Demonstrate use of the broken-record technique for *in vivo* situations. (24, 25)

13. Verbalize an increased understanding of criticism when it is meant as manipulation to conformity. (26)

14. Demonstrate the use of *acknowledgment* as response to accurate criticism. (27, 28, 33)

15. Practice assertive skill of *clouding* in response to manipulative criticism. (29, 30, 31, 32, 33, 34)

16. Practice assertive skill of *probing* to assess the type of criticism being applied. (35, 36, 39, 40)

17. Demonstrate use of *content-to-process shift* during conflict. (37, 38, 39, 40)

18. Practice use of *time-out* when impasse is reached in social conflict resolution. (41, 43, 44)

6. Facilitate group discussion about the nonverbal components of assertive communication (eye contact, body posture, tone of voice, etc.).

7. Have group members identify areas in their lives in which they are most resistant to being assertive, and help them set appropriate (specific, realistic, and observable) goals for themselves.

8. Have group members assess the personal importance of each goal for being assertive, as well as the expected difficulty of achieving each goal.

9. Teach group members the premises underlying each mode of communication: that *assertive* is based on a sense of equal rights, *passive* on a belief that others' rights are more valid than one's own, and *aggressive* on a belief that one's own rights are more important than others'.

10. Develop with group members a list of mistaken traditional assumptions about social relationships (e.g., "You should always accommodate the needs of others," "It's terrible to make mistakes," "It's essential to always be consistent and logical").

11. Help members formulate a list of their personal rights (e.g., "You have the right to

19. Demonstrate the skill of *slowing down* the interaction in the face of criticism. (42, 43, 44)

20. Exhibit use of *assertive position statement*. (45, 46, 47, 49)

21. Demonstrate *active listening skills*. (48, 49)

22. Practice *assertive problem solving*. (50, 51, 52)

23. Acknowledge success in meeting goals in problem areas. (53)

—. _____
_____

—. _____
_____

—. _____
_____

say no"; "You have the right to make mistakes"; "You have the right to change your mind") that counter the traditional assumptions about social relationships.

12. Confront group members who hold onto mistaken traditional beliefs. Explore with these members the origins of those beliefs.

13. Confront group members who cannot accept assertive rights and explore the origins of their resistance.

14. Assign group members to recite daily the list of assertive rights.

15. Elicit from group members general fears about being assertive (e.g., fear of rejection, fear of failure, fear of making a fool of oneself).

16. Help members assess their fears of being assertive in specific situations and replace them with more realistic alternatives. Use specific questions to challenge these fears (e.g., "What is the worst thing that could happen?" "What belief triggers this fear?" "What evidence supports or refutes this belief?" "What might more realistically happen?" "What will happen if I keep on doing as I have?").

17. Give members the questions as a handout, and encourage them in dyads to continue to confront their

fears of being assertive in specific situations.

18. Facilitate group discussion about the process of confronting fears of being assertive.

19. Assign group members to use their questions to confront their fears of being assertive in the problem situations they described earlier.

20. Teach the *broken-record* assertive skill, in which one repeats a brief, clear statement of what he/she wants over and over regardless of opposition, and have members identify situations in their lives where this skill would be appropriate.

21. Lead members through visualization of using the broken-record technique successfully.

22. Have each member role-play the broken-record technique in front of the rest of the group and encourage other group members through modeling to give constructive feedback.

23. Role-play in groups of four the broken-record technique, with two members participating in the role play and two coaching and giving constructive feedback.

24. Assign group members to practice the broken-record technique *in vivo* during the week.

25. Review members' experience with the broken-record technique, reinforcing success and redirecting unsuccessful attempts.

26. Describe a type of criticism that can be a powerful form of manipulation that ensures conformity. Facilitate group discussion of the link between childhood experiences with criticism and adult associations of shame and personal rejection.

27. Teach simple *acknowledgment,* without excuses or apologies ("Yes, you're right, I was late today") as an appropriate response to accurate or constructive feedback versus manipulative criticism.

28. Have group members practice responding to minor criticisms (with which they agree) by acknowledging.

29. Teach the three components of the assertive skill of *clouding* as a response to nonconstructive, manipulative criticism ("You're late again"; "You're always late"; "You're the most disorganized, unreliable person I know"): (1) agree in part ("You're right, I am late tonight"); (2) agree in probability ("You're probably right that I'm often late"); (3) agree in principle ("If everyone were as disorganized and unreliable as you say I am, we'd never get anywhere").

30. Criticize each member of the group in turn, and have them respond by clouding with agreement in part.

31. Criticize each member of the group in turn, and have them respond by clouding with agreement in probability.

32. Criticize each member of the group in turn, and have them respond by clouding with agreement in principle.

33. Assign group members to practice during the week responding to criticism with either acknowledgment or clouding. Have members listen to the criticism that others have experienced and imagine their own responses to the criticism.

34. Review members' experience using acknowledgment or clouding as a response to either constructive or manipulative criticism, reinforcing success and redirecting in cases of failure.

35. Teach group members the skill of *probing* to use when uncertain whether the motives of the critic are constructive or manipulative ("What is it about my being late that bothers you?"). Encourage members to switch to clouding if they determine the criticism is manipulative or to acknowledgment if it is constructive.

36. Role-play, in groups of four, the use of probing, with one member criticizing, another probing, and the other two coaching and giving constructive feedback.

37. Teach the skill of *content-to-process shift* when the conversation goes off track or gets stuck because of conflict ("You seem to be getting angry," or "You're bringing up stuff from the past. That seems beside the point right now.") Explain how to bring the conversation back to the topic at hand.

38. Role-play, in groups of four, the use of content-to-process shift, with one member criticizing, another responding, and the other two coaching and giving constructive feedback.

39. Assign group members to practice the skills of probing and shifting the focus from content to process during the week in response to criticism.

40. Have members report back to the rest of the group their success in using probing and content-to-process shift during the week.

41. Teach the use of *time-out* to allow group members to postpone a conversation until another time.

42. Teach members the skill of *slowing down* an interaction to reduce the pressure

of an instant response (e.g., "I really want to think about this a minute," "This is important, let's slow down," "Wait a minute, could you say that again?").

43. Have group members role-play, in groups of four, the skills of time-out and slowing down, with one member criticizing, another responding, and the other two coaching and giving constructive feedback.

44. Assign members to practice the skills of time-out and slowing down during the week, reporting back to the rest of the group on their success.

45. Facilitate group discussion to clarify distinction between thoughts and feelings.

46. Teach the four components of making *assertive position statements:* (1) describing the situation from own perspective; (2) describing feelings; (3) describing wants; and (4) describing reinforcement to motivate cooperation (or consequence of noncooperation).

47. Demonstrate to group members several assertive position statements.

48. Teach the three components of *active listening:* (1) listening with full attention; (2) listening to the feelings as well as the content; (3) acknowledging receipt of the

message through para-
phrasing.

49. Have members role-play in
groups of four, with one
making an assertive posi-
tion statement, another
using active listening, and
the other two coaching and
giving feedback.

50. Teach the five basic steps to
assertive problem solving:
(1) defining the problem; (2)
listing alternative solutions
based on each person's feelings and wants; (3) reviewing and eliminating
mutually intolerable alternatives; (4) picking an acceptable compromise
solution and a backup plan;
(5) evaluating success.

51. Have members role-play assertive problem solving and
facilitate discussion of any
difficulties encountered.

52. Assign members to practice
assertive problem solving
during the week and review
success.

53. Review members' original
problem areas and assess
success in meeting goals.

__. _____

_____

__. _____

_____

__. _____

_____

DIAGNOSTIC SUGGESTIONS

Axis I: 300.00   Anxiety Disorder NOS
              300.23   Social Phobia
              296.xx   Major Depressive Disorder
              300.4   Dysthymic Disorder

              _____   _____

              _____   _____

Axis II: 301.82   Avoidant Personality Disorder
              301.7   Antisocial Personality Disorder
              301.6   Dependent Personality Disorder

              _____   _____

              _____   _____

BULIMIA

BEHAVIORAL DEFINITIONS

1. Rapid consumption of large quantities of food in a short time followed by self-induced vomiting due to fear of weight gain.
2. Preoccupation with food, weight, and appearance.
3. Physiological symptoms of eating disorder, including digestive problems, erosion of dental enamel, increased cavities, electrolyte imbalance, irregular or no menstrual cycles, and dehydration.
4. Feelings of depression, anxiety, fear, or anger.
5. Feelings of low self-esteem that predate the bulimic behavior.
6. Increased sensitivity to criticism and approval.
7. Feelings of shame leading to social withdrawal and isolation.
8. No substance abuse disorder.

—. _____
_____

—. _____
_____

—. _____
_____

LONG-TERM GOALS

1. Develop a sense of hope about the future and the possibility of long-term recovery.
2. Terminate the pattern of binge eating and vomiting, and develop a range of behavioral alternatives.
3. Decrease feelings of shame and guilt and the associated isolation.
4. Increase feelings of self-esteem.
5. Reduce physiological symptoms of eating disorder.

—. _____

_____

—. _____

_____

—. _____

_____

SHORT-TERM OBJECTIVES

1. Describe behavior that led to seeking treatment for an eating disorder. (1)

2. Verbalize an increased understanding of bulimia as a coping strategy for uncomfortable feelings. (2, 3)

3. Verbalize expectations about the outcome of group treatment of eating disorders. (4, 5, 6)

4. Verbalize an increased understanding of crash or severe dieting as an unsuccessful weight-loss strategy and a potential trigger for bulimic behavior. (7, 8)

5. Monitor eating patterns and binge triggers in a food journal. (9, 10, 11, 12)

6. State the distinction between physical and emotional hunger, and relate personal experiences that demonstrate the interplay. (13, 14, 15)

7. Keep a journal describing *in vivo* experiences of physical hunger and emotional hunger. (16, 17, 18)

THERAPEUTIC INTERVENTIONS

1. Have members introduce themselves and describe their history of binge-purge behaviors, preoccupation with food, and other reasons for attending the group.

2. Describe to the group the way bulimia works to reduce uncomfortable feelings (tension, self-hatred, anxiety, depression, anger, etc.)

3. Elicit from group members personal examples that confirm bulimia as a coping strategy.

4. Facilitate group discussion about what members expect as a result of group treatment of their eating disorder.

5. Model and encourage nonjudgmental support for positive expectations of treatment that will result in significant behavioral change.

6. Remind members of the hard work involved in recovering from bulimia, soliciting individual

8. Verbalize realistic, specific, and manageable short-term behavioral goals. (19, 22, 23)

9. Demonstrate successful completion of behavioral goals. (20, 21, 23)

10. Verbalize an increased understanding of the pattern of categorizing food as either good or bad and the influence of this categorization on bulimic behavior. (24, 25)

11. Decrease categorization of food as either good or bad, and eat a "bad" food without purging. (26, 27)

12. Clarify distinction between enough food and too much food. (28, 29)

13. Identify specific feelings experienced and any physiological concomitants. (30, 31, 32, 33)

14. Identify negative, critical cognitions that trigger bingeing and purging. (34)

15. Replace negative, critical cognitions with self-affirming, reality-based cognitions. (35, 36, 37, 38)

16. List alternative behaviors that can be used to cope with uncomfortable emotions to replace the binge-purge cycle as the negative coping response. (39, 40, 41)

17. Report on instances of increased tolerance of uncomfortable emotions. (41)

commitments to follow through with treatment.

7. Teach group members how deprivation associated with crash or severe dieting triggers binge behavior and maintains bulimia.

8. Share with group members the statistics showing crash dieting as an unsuccessful weight-loss strategy.

9. Assign group members to keep a food journal, monitoring time of day, location, whether they were alone or with others, how physically hungry they were on a scale of 1 to 5, feelings before eating, what was eaten or drunk, how much of it was satisfying, thoughts occurring before it became a binge (if relevant), and thoughts after finishing eating.

10. Elicit group members' feelings about keeping a food journal.

11. Review members' food journals and encourage members to share insights or problems with the rest of the group.

12. Model and encourage group members to practice supportive feedback to each other regarding keeping a thorough, consistent journal.

13. Teach the concept that emotional hunger resulting from unacknowledged feelings is different from physical hunger.

18. Demonstrate increased assertiveness by verbalizing requests for help. (42, 43, 44, 45)

19. Demonstrate increased assertiveness by setting limits and maintaining boundaries. (46, 47, 48, 49)

20. Cooperate with a full physical exam. (50)

21. Cooperate with a dental exam. (51)

___. _____
    _____

___. _____
    _____

___. _____
    _____

14. Explain that people with bulimia rarely experience physical hunger because bingeing and purging interferes with normal hunger cycles.

15. Encourage group members to share personal experiences of responding to emotional feelings as they would to physical hunger.

16. Have group members identify where in their bodies they experience physical hunger.

17. Assign group members to use their food journals to differentiate between physical and emotional hunger.

18. Review members' success in distinguishing physical from emotional hunger.

19. Have each group member state a goal he or she would like to accomplish during the week, not necessarily related to food, but of emotional significance. Help each member shape a goal that is behaviorally specific, manageable, and realistic (e.g., "I want to be nicer to my sister" might shape into "I want to call my sister and tell her that I love her"; "I want to be binge-free during work hours on Friday" rather than "I want to stop bingeing").

20. Assign group members to fulfill their goals during the week and to report on their successes in doing so.

21. Encourage group discussion about the goal exercise, giving and eliciting from other members supportive feedback.

22. Assign group members to set weekly goals about food intake that are specific, realistic, and manageable.

23. Review members' successes and difficulties in achieving weekly goals.

24. Explore with group members the characteristic categorization of food into "good" and "bad." Elicit from members personal examples of the impact on self-esteem (and on bulimic behavior) of eating something "bad."

25. Facilitate group discussion about the pressure to purge after eating even a small amount of "bad" food and the accompanying tendency to binge on that "bad" food first.

26. Assign group members to challenge the good/bad dichotomy by moving one marginal food out of the "bad" category, eating some of it without purging (or bingeing). Predict high anxiety as a result of this change.

27. Review members' success in eating some "bad" food and tolerating the anxiety and pressure to purge.

28. Assign group members to monitor and journal when they have eaten enough but not too much of any food during the week.

29. Have members share their experiences and insights about their eating patterns with respect to the "enough but not too much" issue.

30. Explain to group members that responding to uncomfortable feelings in nonbulimic ways requires the ability to identify specific feelings and to develop alternative coping strategies.

31. Help members during group discussion identify the specific feelings experienced and any physiological concomitants of those feelings.

32. Give each group member a list of 100 common feelings and ask them to monitor, identify, and record their feelings during the week, using the list as a reference.

33. Review and discuss group members' experience with monitoring their feelings, reinforcing successful differentiation of emotions.

34. Teach group members the causal link between thoughts and feelings. Help them identify their own self-critical thoughts that trigger negative feelings.

35. Teach group members thought-stopping techniques

(e.g., mentally shouting "Stop" or snapping a rubber band around the wrist).

36. Assign members to identify negative, self-critical cognitions during the week and practice thought-stopping techniques.

37. Have members report back to the rest of the group on their success in using thought-stopping techniques, reinforcing success at negative thought avoidance.

38. Help group members develop positive, reality-based, self-affirming cognitions to replace the negative cognitions.

39. Facilitate group discussion of positive alternative strategies of coping with uncomfortable emotions to replace the negative coping response of binge-purge behavior.

40. Encourage members to share personal examples that have worked for them as ways to cope with uncomfortable feelings, including predicting and avoiding binge triggers.

41. Stress the need for tolerating some feelings until they pass—without bingeing or purging—when there seems to be no strategy for addressing them (e.g., loneliness when it's too late to call someone; anger when

there's no self-critical trigger thought).

42. Teach group members the concept of asking for help as a strategy in recovery from bulimia. Model asking for help in clear, direct, assertive ways.

43. Have group members role-play in dyads, asking for help in situations where they have difficulty asking.

44. Facilitate group discussion about the experience of asking for help.

45. Assign group members to ask three people for help with something significant during the week; review results with the rest of the group, reinforcing successful assertiveness.

46. Teach group members how the frustration and anger that result from the inability to say no and set limits is a major binge trigger.

47. Elicit individual examples of situations in which members said yes when they would have liked to say no.

48. Have group members role-play in dyads, saying no about something of significance in their lives.

49. Assign members to say no three times during the week in response to requests and then report back to the rest of the group on the experience.

50. Refer to physician for physical exam.

51. Refer to dentist for dental exam.

—. _____

_____

—. _____

_____

—. _____

_____

DIAGNOSTIC SUGGESTIONS

Axis I: 307.51   Bulimia Nervosa

_____   _____

_____   _____

Axis II: 301.6   Dependent Personality Disorder

_____   _____

_____   _____

CAREGIVER BURNOUT

BEHAVIORAL DEFINITIONS

1. Primary responsibility for the care and well-being of a person disabled by chronic illness, debilitating disease, or age.
2. Responsibility for a disabled person that exceeds own abilities to cope effectively and results in impairment in work or relationship functioning.
3. Tendency to feel exhausted, angry, guilty, resentful, or helpless.
4. Fear of attending to immediate family members' needs less than adequately because of responsibilities for disabled person.
5. Feelings of grief associated with the ongoing experience of loss.

—. _____
   _____
—. _____
   _____
—. _____
   _____

LONG-TERM GOALS

1. Assess needs of disabled person and necessity for/availability of outside assistance.
2. Increase ability to meet own needs and those of immediate family members.
3. Make contingency plans for the future care of the disabled person should his/her situation change or illness progress.
4. Improve functioning at work and harmony in relationships.
5. Reduce resentment and increase acceptance of role as caregiver and resulting limitations while working to reduce limitations.

6. Reduce feelings of guilt, anger, helplessness, and isolation.
7. Express the grief associated with the ongoing loss of the disabled person.

—. _____

_____

—. _____

_____

—. _____

_____

SHORT-TERM OBJECTIVES

1. Verbalize the stresses and frustrations surrounding the role of being a caregiver. (1, 3)

2. Describe responsibilities as caregiver and medical condition of disabled person, including prognosis for change. (2, 3)

3. Identify impact of caregiving responsibilities on self and family. (3, 4, 5)

4. Express feelings about caregiving responsibilities and their effects on own family life. (6, 7)

5. Verbalize the changes in roles required by the caregiving situation. (8)

6. List alternative outside resources and their potential incorporation into daily routines. (9, 10, 11)

7. Verbalize a resolution of feelings of guilt associated with utilizing outside re-

THERAPEUTIC INTERVENTIONS

1. Ask each group member to describe his/her current caregiving situation and the stresses that prompted joining the group.

2. Encourage members' sharing of the medical conditions of the persons for whom they care and the responsibilities they assume as caregivers. Have them include any known information about the future course of the disability.

3. Facilitate group discussion of the stresses involved (emotional drain, time demands, financial strain, etc.) in being a caregiver.

4. Elicit from group members how being a caregiver positively and negatively impacts career, personal life, and relationships with friends and family members.

5. Help group members identify the positive and nega-

sources for caregiving assistance. (12)

8. Prioritize necessary versus unnecessary tasks, and implement these priorities in managing time and behavior during the week. (13, 14, 15)

9. Verbalize understanding that the disabled person's well-being depends directly on own well-being. (16)

10. Demonstrate an increase in the frequency of the implementation of self-nurturing activities. (17, 18)

11. Verbalize plans for future care of the disabled person if the disability progresses. (2, 19)

12. Increase participation in social activities and interactions to reduce isolation. (20, 21, 22)

13. Identify needs of children involved in caregiving situation and evaluate ways of best meeting their needs. (23)

14. Verbalize commitment to ongoing self-care as a balance to caregiving responsibilities. (24)

15. Report a reduction in feelings of isolation, frustration, guilt, helplessness, and depression as changes are made in caregiving pattern. (6, 12, 25)

tive impact on own children of having a disabled person in the extended family or even in their home.

6. Encourage members' appropriate expression of feelings (including anger, resentment, guilt, helplessness) associated with being a caregiver.

7. Demonstrate and facilitate group members' expression of empathetic support for speaker.

8. Facilitate group exploration of the role changes involved in some caregiving situations, including the emotional impact of parenting a parent.

9. Encourage group members' exchange of information about outside resources for respite care of the disabled. Provide additional material, or assign members to search for additional resources when necessary.

10. Facilitate individual members strategizing ways of incorporating outside resources into their daily lives as a means of reducing own stress.

11. Assign members to use at least one additional resource during the week and report back to the group on their successes.

12. Elicit from group members the feelings of guilt that arise from recognizing own

—.   _____
     _____
—.   _____
     _____
—.   _____

limitations and the resulting need to ask for help; encourage group members to support each other in utilizing other sources of caregiving help.

13. Have each group member write a detailed list of the responsibilities and tasks he/she completes (or attempts to complete) on a daily basis.

14. Teach group members the three-drawer approach to prioritizing responsibilities, where top-drawer tasks are the essential ones, middle-drawer tasks include those that can endure a temporary postponement without negative consequences, and bottom-drawer tasks are those that can be shelved indefinitely.

15. Assign group members to prioritize their daily task lists during the week and focus on completing only top-drawer responsibilities. Have members report back to the group on their success in prioritizing.

16. Facilitate group discussion about the concept that the disabled person's well-being is directly related to the well-being of the caregiver.

17. Encourage group members to make personal lists of self-nurturing activities (e.g., taking a warm bath, listening to music, reading a good book).

18. Assign group members to include at least one self-nurturing activity on their top-drawer task list every day, and review their success at implementation of these self-nurturing activities.

19. Assist group members in planning for the future care of their patients should changes occur in the patient's medical conditions.

20. With their permission, provide members with a list of the names and phone numbers of all group members, and assign them to call at least one person from the group during the week.

21. Assign group members to participate in at least one social interaction/activity with someone outside the home or group during the week. Ensure that the activity be placed on the top-drawer task list.

22. Review group members' experiences participating in social interactions. Reinforce successful experiences and gently confront resistance.

23. Facilitate group discussion about the needs of own children involved in caregiving situations. Discuss members' attempts to best meet those needs, and strategize alternative means.

24. Assist group members in developing a plan for ongoing self-care, including asking for help, prioritizing

daily responsibilities, doing self-nurturing activities, and avoiding isolation.

25. Acknowledge and reinforce positive changes in caregiving pattern and in the resolution of negative feelings associated with caregiving.

__. _____

_____

__. _____

_____

__. _____

_____

DIAGNOSTIC SUGGESTIONS

Axis I:

296.2x	Major Depressive Disorder, Single Episode
300.4	Dysthymic Disorder
300.02	Generalized Anxiety Disorder
309.0	Adjustment Disorder With Depressed Mood
309.24	Adjustment Disorder With Anxiety
309.28	Adjustment Disorder With Mixed Anxiety and Depressed Mood

_____   _____

_____   _____

CHEMICAL DEPENDENCE

BEHAVIORAL DEFINITIONS

1. Maladaptive pattern of mood-altering substance use manifested by increased tolerance and withdrawal.
2. Inability to stop or cut own use of mood-altering drug despite the verbalized desire to do so and the negative consequences of continued use.
3. Blood work (elevated liver enzymes, electrolyte imbalance, etc.) and physical indicators (stomach pain, high blood pressure, malnutrition, etc.) reflect a pattern of heavy alcohol abuse.
4. Frequent blackouts when abusing alcohol.
5. Continued mood-altering substance abuse despite persistent physical, legal, financial, vocational, social, or relationship problems that are directly caused by the substance abuse.
6. Drug tolerance increases as increased substance use is required to become intoxicated or to recall the desired effect.
7. Physical withdrawal symptoms (shaking, seizures, nausea, headaches, sweating, anxiety, insomnia, and/or depression) when the body is deprived of the addictive substance for any length of time.
8. Arrests for substance abuse–related offenses (e.g., driving under the influence, minor in possession, assault, possession/delivery of a controlled substance, shoplifting).
9. Suspension of important social, recreational, or occupational activities because they interfere with the use of the mood-altering drug.
10. Large time investment in activities related to obtaining the mood-altering substance, using it, or recovering from its effects.
11. Consumption of the mood-altering substance in greater amounts and for longer periods than intended.
12. Continued use of mood-altering chemical despite physician's warning that it is causing health problems.
13. At least some acknowledgment that chemical dependence is a problem.

—. _____
_____
—. _____
_____
—. _____
_____

LONG-TERM GOALS

1. Accept chemical dependence and the resulting powerlessness over and unmanageability of mood-altering substances.
2. Establish a sustained recovery, free from the use of all mood-altering substances.
3. Establish and maintain total abstinence from all mood-altering drugs while increasing knowledge of addiction and the recovery process.
4. Acquire the necessary skills to maintain long-term sobriety from all mood-altering substances.
5. Improve quality of life by maintaining abstinence from all mood-altering chemicals.
6. Withdraw from mood-altering substance, stabilize physically and emotionally, and then establish a supportive recovery plan.

—. _____
_____
—. _____
_____
—. _____
_____

SHORT-TERM OBJECTIVES

1. Verbalize a precipitating substance abuse event that led to participation in the group. (1, 2)

THERAPEUTIC INTERVENTIONS

1. Ask each member to describe a particular substance abuse incident that

2. Identify the negative effects substance abuse has had on life. (2, 3)

3. Demonstrate decreased denial regarding chemical dependence by making fewer statements minimizing the frequency, amount, and seriousness of use and its negative impact. (3, 28)

4. Verbally acknowledge substance use as a choice. (4, 7, 8, 9, 33)

5. Identify own position in the five stages of addiction and recovery. (5, 6, 7)

6. Verbalize an increased understanding of physiological and psychological addiction. (10, 11)

7. Identify the different categories of drugs and their method of use. (12, 13, 14)

8. Give examples of how denial has contributed to continuing substance abuse. (15, 17)

9. Identify behavioral alternatives to getting high over the weekend. (16, 17)

10. Identify behavioral and social triggers for substance use. (18)

11. Identify alternative coping behaviors and thoughts to deal with social and environmental triggers for relapse. (19)

12. Demonstrate the skill to relax without the use of drugs. (20)

motivated participation in the group.

2. Have each member describe his or her history of substance use, including drug of choice, amount and pattern of use, and negative life consequences resulting from chemical dependence.

3. Confront—and facilitate confrontation by other members of—speaker's denial, minimization, or rationalization of the seriousness of substance abuse problem.

4. Stress to group members that using or abusing alcohol and drugs is a matter of choice: the long-term choice for sobriety and the every-minute-of-every-day choice to not use.

5. Give each member a copy of "Five Days in the Life of an Addict" by Peter D. Rogers (found in *Focal Group Psychotherapy* by McKay and Paleg), and describe the five stages of addiction and recovery: identifying self as a helpless victim; denial of the problem and responsibility for it; acceptance of responsibility for having a "bad habit"; decision to act responsibly in the face of problem; making new choices to avoid problem altogether.

6. Elicit from members examples of situations reflecting their personal stage of addiction or recovery.

13. Identify major stressors in life that contribute to substance use. (21)

14. List positive alternatives to substance abuse as a means of coping with stressful life-change events. (22)

15. Describe the roles children adopt in alcoholic families, and identify role taken in own family of origin. (23, 24)

16. Give examples from daily life of increased use of direct, assertive statements to express needs and personal desires. (25, 26, 27)

17. Identify potential emotional relapse triggers and verbalize strategies for dealing with each one. (28, 29, 30)

18. Identify distorted, negative thoughts that trigger relapse and/or support denial. (31)

19. Report on implementing positive, realistic thoughts to replace negative cognitions. (32)

20. Verbalize an understanding of five stages that lead to changing problem behaviors. (33)

21. Identify own specific stage of change presently achieved. (34)

22. List the pros and cons of terminating substance abuse. (35)

23. Identify steps necessary to achieve a high level of confidence regarding resisting temptation to relapse. (36)

7. Facilitate group discussion of a point in each member's life where making a different choice would have resulted in not using.

8. Assign group members to observe the choices they make during the week that increase or decrease their chances of using.

9. Review members' observations of their choices, reinforcing successful avoidance of use while confronting and redirecting choices that result in substance use.

10. Reframe relapse as an inevitable part of the recovery *process.*

11. Explain the concepts of tolerance and withdrawal as applied to addictive substance abuse.

12. Solicit group members' knowledge to develop a list of the variety of drugs of abuse, broken down into three categories: "uppers," "downers," and "sideways" (psychedelics or hallucinogens). Then facilitate discussion of the short- and long-term effects of the various drugs.

13. Stress that drugs themselves are neither bad nor good; rather, abuse of the drugs is the problem.

14. Teach group members that while all of the drugs have their use in certain situations, none provide anything

24. Verbalize life changes necessary for maintaining sobriety. (37, 38)

25. Verbalize a plan for activating necessary life changes and maintaining long-term sobriety. (39)

26. Identify potential sources of ongoing caring and support in maintaining sobriety. (39, 40)

__. _____
   _____

__. _____
   _____

__. _____
   _____

in terms of mood alteration that can't be achieved using nondrug alternatives (albeit more slowly and with more effort).

15. Facilitate group discussion about the impact of denial on individual member's substance use and abuse.

16. Using examples from group members, develop a comprehensive list of constructive, healthy activities that would keep them busy during the weekend.

17. Explore with group members potential problems (including denial) that might arise as they try to participate in constructive activities without using substances, and help members formulate strategies for dealing with these problems.

18. Assign group members to record the "slippery" (high risk of "slipping," or relapsing) places and people in their lives.

19. Solicit options for coping with people or places that trigger relapse for each member.

20. Teach deep-breathing and progressive relaxation to group members and encourage them to practice at least once during the week, preferably daily.

21. Ask each group member to identify, using the Holmes and Rahe stress chart, the

major life-change events that have occurred in the last two years. Add additional stress events to the chart if necessary.

22. Teach that all change, positive and negative, is stressful, and facilitate group discussion of the life stressors each member has experienced. Encourage group brainstorming of alternative ways of coping with stressful situations without using a mood-altering substance.

23. Teach group members the roles (see *Another Chance* by Wegscheider) usually adopted by children of alcoholic parents (e.g., the family hero, the scapegoat, the lost child, the mascot). Help members identify the role (or roles) each took in his/her family of origin.

24. Have each group member contact close friends and family members to confirm the role the member took in his/her family of origin and report back to the group the following week.

25. Facilitate group discussion about the distinction between passive, aggressive, and assertive communication between partners. Explore how assertive communication of thoughts and feelings may reduce the urge for substance abuse.

26. Using role playing and be-havioral rehearsal, have group members practice making assertive state-ments.

27. Assign members to practice being assertive during the week, and review members' progress the following week.

28. Confront any member's con-tinual slips as a sign of in-sufficient commitment and set limit of "three slips and you're out."

29. Explain the HALT acronym (*h*ungry, *a*ngry, *l*onely, *t*ired) describing the emotional states that hold potential relapse danger. Help group members identify means of coping positively with those emotional states.

30. Explore with group mem-bers the common cognitive and behavioral pitfalls to recovery (e.g., lengthy fan-tasies about using; dishon-esty with self or others; excessive expectations; ex-treme self-assurance; stop-ping activities that sustain sobriety, such as relaxation, AA attendance, exercise), and discuss strategies for avoiding them.

31. Assist members in identify-ing distorted, negative cog-nitions that can trigger relapse or nurture denial.

32. Help group members list positive, realistic thoughts to replace distorted cogni-tions; review the use of

these positive thoughts in daily life.

33. Teach the following five stages of change identified by the Transtheoretical Model (Prochaska, Di-Clemente, and Norcross) as necessary for people to successfully modify problem behaviors such as addictions: *precontemplation* (not planning on changing); *contemplation* (considering change in the next six months); *preparation* (getting ready to change in the next month); *action* (currently changing); and *maintenance* (maintaining change for at least six months).

34. Assists each group member in identifying which stage of change they are in and what is necessary to move to the next stage.

35. Solicit from group members the pros and cons of terminating substance abuse.

36. Assist each member in identifying his/her degree of confidence in resisting temptation to relapse and what steps are necessary to increase that degree of confidence.

37. Assist group members in developing "maps" to emphasize "choice points" in their lives. (For example, when driving to work, there's a critical point at which a member can choose to drive

past the corner bar or pick a different route; there's a point in the hallway at work where a member may choose either to visit the bathroom in which "doing a line" is common or move on to a different bathroom.)

38. Help group members identify the specific life changes each will need to make to maintain sobriety (e.g., implement positive and realistic thoughts, continue relaxation exercises, attend long-term support group such as AA or NA, find and maintain clean/sober friends).

39. Facilitate discussion of specific steps members can take to implement their needed life changes.

40. Encourage group members to stay in touch with each other as a source of ongoing support and caring in maintaining sobriety.

___. _____

_____

___. _____

_____

___. _____

_____

DIAGNOSTIC SUGGESTIONS

Axis I: 303.90   Alcohol Dependence
305.00   Alcohol Abuse
304.30   Cannabis Dependence
305.20   Cannabis Abuse
304.20   Cocaine Dependence
305.60   Cocaine Abuse
304.80   Polysubstance Dependence
304.10   Sedative, Hypnotic, or Anxiolytic Dependence
V71.01   Adult Antisocial Behavior

_____   _____

_____   _____

Axis II: 301.7   Antisocial Personality Disorder

_____   _____

_____   _____

CHILD MOLESTER—ADOLESCENT

BEHAVIORAL DEFINITIONS

1. Sexual contact with a younger child with whom client has a close or trusting relationship.
2. Inappropriate sexual "noncontact" (voyeurism, exhibitionism, obscene phone calls) with a younger child with whom client has a close or trusting relationship.
3. Recognition that the offending behavior is inappropriate.
4. Admission of responsibility for at least some aspect of the alleged sexual abuse.
5. Blaming of the victim or the circumstances for the sexual contact.
6. Major cognitive distortions about victim resulting in rationalizing the sexual abuse.
7. Underdeveloped empathic skills.
8. Inability to establish and maintain meaningful friendships.
9. Feelings of low self-esteem.
10. Not an adolescent rapist or sexual compulsive.
11. Concurrent willingness to participate in individual and family therapy.
12. Parent of adolescent child molester.

—. _____
_____

—. _____
_____

—. _____
_____

LONG-TERM GOALS

1. Acknowledge personal responsibility for own inappropriate sexual behavior and terminate sexual abuse.
2. Break through the denial associated with the offending behavior and develop honesty with self and others.
3. Develop empathy with respect to the effects of the sexual abuse on the victim.
4. Understand the factors that led to the offending behavior and develop skills to prevent it from recurring.
5. Enter into and remain in individual and family therapy.
6. Develop appropriate relationships with friends.
7. Develop coping strategies that minimize the risk of relapse.

—. _____

   _____

—. _____

   _____

—. _____

   _____

SHORT-TERM OBJECTIVES

1. Verbalize the details of the adolescent sexual offenses that led to participation in the group treatment. (1, 2)

2. Increase understanding of the possible legal and other consequences that lie ahead. (3)

3. Verbalize the factors that made the sexual behavior abusive and inappropriate. (4, 5)

4. Verbally compare the facts of their sexual abuse behavior with the commonly accepted myths of sexual abuse. (6)

THERAPEUTIC INTERVENTIONS

1. Ask each member to describe in detail his offenses or his/her son's offenses.

2. Facilitate group confrontation of any speaker's denial, rationalization, and minimization of his (or his/her son's) sexually abusive behavior.

3. Teach the variety of possible outcomes for adolescent offenders vis-à-vis the criminal justice system.

4. Explain the factors that make sexual behavior between two people abusive (e.g., age differences, threat

5. Verbalize an understanding of how sexual abuse occurs as a result of unresolved childhood issues and conflicts not necessarily related to sexual issues. (7)

6. Identify early painful loss or abuse experiences, including those related to parental alcoholism or drug abuse. (8, 9)

7. Identify the negative thoughts and feelings that accompany memories of childhood abuse. (10)

8. Identify the ways the thoughts and feelings associated with childhood abuse affect current behavior. (11, 12)

9. Keep a journal of daily stressful events and thoughts, feelings, and fantasies related to sexual abuse. (13)

10. Identify the events—usually involving a significant other person or life stress—that trigger high-risk feelings of hurt, anger, helplessness, and anxiety similar to those associated with unresolved family conflicts or earlier abuses. (13)

11. Identify and confront the distorted thoughts about the abuse that occur before, during, and after the abuse and that justify the behavior. (14, 15)

12. Verbalize realistic cognitions about sexual abuse

of physical harm, misuse of trust).

5. Ask group members to identify and discuss the factors involved in their own or their sons' sexual offenses.

6. Discuss with group members the myths of sexual abuse (e.g., abusers must be "crazy"; abusers don't know their victims) and have members compare these myths with the realities of their own or their son's offenses.

7. Describe to the group the chain of events showing links between childhood abuse (physical, emotional, and sexual), the painful emotions and cognitions that result, the current adolescent triggers of those painful emotions and cognitions, and the current coping strategies that lead to offending behavior.

8. Assign adolescent members to list and share with the rest of the group childhood abuses that can still arouse emotional pain.

9. Demonstrate and facilitate the expression of empathy with the speaker about the pain associated with his early abuses.

10. Help group members identify the negative thoughts and feelings associated with the early abuses. Encourage members to compare and contrast their own thoughts

and the victim that avoid high-risk distortions. (16)

13. Verbalize characteristics common to adolescent offenders and their victims. (17)

14. Verbalize an understanding of how sex can be an expression of power or control versus love and affection. (18)

15. Identify ongoing sexual thoughts regarding the victim. (19)

16. Report on the implementation of thought-stopping techniques to control inappropriate fantasies. (19, 20)

17. Replace negative thoughts about self with positive, self-affirming thought patterns. (21)

18. Verbalize the intent to terminate all sexual abuse and to not indulge associated fantasies. (22)

19. Acknowledge that knowing sexual abuse is wrong is not enough to prevent its recurrence, and identify other critical elements necessary for successful termination of sex abuse. (23)

20. Identify the chain of events involved in the relapse process that leads to reoffenses. (24)

21. Identify and remove external stimuli that trigger relapse. (25)

22. Report on the successful implementation of escape

and feelings with those of the speaker.

11. Ask group members to explore with each other whether and how the thoughts and feelings that occur before each current sexual offense are the same as those associated with their childhood experiences of abuse.

12. Assist adolescent group members in identifying the strategies they use in coping with negative thoughts and feelings that result in sexual offending.

13. Assign adolescent members to keep daily journals of their thoughts, feelings, and fantasies of sexual abuse, including the stressful events that were happening around them before sexual thoughts or fantasies occurred; process journal material, identifying trigger events for sexually inappropriate thoughts.

14. Have group members identify and discuss the cognitive distortions used to justify the sexual offenses (e.g., "I'm just curious, I'm not hurting anyone," "_____ did it to me, so it must be okay," "I'll only do this once, never again").

15. Facilitate group confrontation of the speaker's inconsistencies in thinking when cognitive distortions are used to justify sexual abuse.

strategies when relapse risk is high. (26, 27)

23. Practice the use of preventive cognitive self-talk during times of high risk for relapse. (28)

24. Verbalize the myths that perpetrators hold about their victims. (29)

25. Verbalize an increased understanding of the common emotional, behavioral, psychological, and physical reactions of victims of abuse. (30, 31)

26. Accurately express the immediate and long-term feelings of the victim of sexual abuse. (32, 33)

27. Verbalize accurate information regarding appropriate, normal sexual development of children and adolescents. (34)

28. Verbalize the difference between consent and coercion associated with sexual behavior. (35)

29. Discuss the abuse with own family members (or parents only, if the victim was not a member of perpetrator's family) and then make appropriate apologies to both the victim and other family members. (36, 37)

30. Express vulnerable feelings, private thoughts, and sexual fantasies. (13, 38, 39)

31. Decrease time spent in isolation and increase fre-

16. Assist group members in developing reality-based cognitions (e.g., "This behavior is wrong and will hurt this person"; "I'm a worthwhile person, I don't need to behave this way to feel okay") to counter and replace the high-risk cognitive distortions.

17. Teach group members the characteristics common to adolescent offenders and their victims (e.g., four of ten victims are members of the offender's family, usually a sibling or cousin; three of ten victims are male, seven female; one of ten victims are strangers to the offender; offenders use verbal coercion more than threats of violence; have members identify those factors relevant to their own offenses.

18. Teach that sexual abuse is an expression of power and control and then ask each group member (offender and parent) to share his or her view of sex as an expression of love and closeness as opposed to power or dominance.

19. Monitor each adolescent's continuing sexual fantasies about the victim, pointing out the danger of indulging such fantasies and encouraging the use of thought-stopping techniques (e.g., visualizing a stop sign,

quency of social contacts. (40, 41)

32. Implement assertiveness skills in the pursuit of meeting previously unmet needs. (42)

33. Verbalize the basic steps involved in problem solving and report on their application to specific conflicts in personal life. (43)

34. Verbalize an understanding of the six elements of anger management through the use of time-out and then practice the use of time-out techniques to modulate anger. (44)

—. _____

_____

—. _____

_____

—. _____

_____

shouting "Stop" to self, replacing thoughts with alternative pleasant, appropriate ones).

20. Review and reinforce successful use of thought-stopping techniques to control inappropriate fantasies.

21. Explore with the group the negative cognitive messages about self that trigger feelings of worthlessness, and facilitate the development of alternative positive cognitions that build self-esteem.

22. Ask each adolescent group member to make explicit his intent to terminate all sexual abuse and to not indulge associated fantasies.

23. Emphasize the need for a multifaceted program (e.g., support group participation, cognitive changes brought about through therapy, strict boundaries on relationships, avoidance of trigger situations) that supports termination of sexual abuse, not just a verbal pledge.

24. Describe the chain of events involved in the relapse process that leads to reoffenses. (For example, past hurts or abuses lead to negative feelings and thoughts about oneself, which result in the high-risk situations of rejection or humiliation that trigger the same nega-

tive thoughts and feelings, which induce coping mechanisms such as alcohol use to deal with the negative thoughts and feelings that facilitate the abuse, which in turn allow cognitive distortions about the victim and about the offending behavior that cause the abuse.) Encourage group members to identify and discuss the chain of events that led to their own or their son's personal relapse.

25. Ask group members to identify and commit to remove the external stimuli in their lives that facilitate relapse (e.g., child pornography, babysitting jobs). Have members report on their compliance to the group.

26. Engage group members in the development and rehearsal of escape strategies to use early in the relapse chain of events (e.g., using thought-stopping strategies; replacing negative cognitions with positive, self-affirming cognitions; physically removing self from the high-risk situation).

27. Review and reinforce group members' use of successful escape strategies to avoid relapse into sexual abuse.

28. Teach how the perceived need for immediate gratification of sexual urges can be controlled through the

development of cognitive self-talk (e.g., "Two minutes of power are not worth time in a juvenile hall"; "I'll feel more ashamed of myself if I abuse this child"; "The victim will never forget the emotional pain of the abuse").

29. Teach and discuss myths that perpetrators hold regarding victims (e.g., "If she doesn't resist, it isn't abuse"; "She really likes it as much as I do"; "She knows it's a way to show that I love her"; "She's too young to remember anything").

30. Assign group members to read and discuss excerpts written by victims of sexual abuse about the painful consequences of being abused.

31. Discuss with members the common reactions of victims to sexual abuse.

32. Facilitate the development of empathy for their victims by using role-reversal techniques to get perpetrator to express the feelings of the victim.

33. Have each adolescent member write about the incest experience from the child victim's perspective. Have members read their papers aloud to the group.

34. Elicit group members' ideas and opinions about normal sexual behavior for children and adolescents, including

the role of sexual fantasies. Correct false information.

35. Clarify the differences between obtaining consent, using coercion, and grooming (or manipulating) a victim; help group members identify and discuss their own use of coercion and grooming in their offending behavior.

36. Ask each adolescent group member to write appropriate apologies to his own family, his victim, and the victim's family (if victim is not a member of offender's family). Have members read their apologies aloud in the group before sharing them with victim or family members.

37. Assign each adolescent member to meet with his own and his victim's families (if different) and explain the chain of events, verbally accepting responsibility for his abusive behavior and making a verbal commitment to act differently in the future. After discussion with family, have the member read aloud his apologies that were written within the group treatment setting.

38. Facilitate appropriate, honest communication between group members.

39. Facilitate expression of feelings among group members.

40. Assign small groups of members to practice social skills exercises and role-play conversations; reinforce social skill improvement.

41. Have group members practice maintaining eye contact while speaking; reinforce success.

42. Ask group members to clarify the distinction between assertion and aggression. Teach basic assertiveness skills and have members practice in small groups.

43. Teach problem-solving skills (e.g., identify problems, brainstorm all possible options, evaluate each option and eliminate mutually intolerable options, select best remaining option, implement course of action, and evaluate results); role-play their application to everyday life conflicts.

44. Explain each of the six components of the time-out technique (*self-monitoring* for escalating feelings of anger and hurt, *signaling* to the other person that verbal engagement should end, *acknowledging* the need of the other person to disengage, *separating* to disengage, *cooling down* to regain control of anger, and *returning* to controlled verbal engagement).

___.   _____

        _____

___.   _____

        _____

___.   _____

        _____

DIAGNOSTIC SUGGESTIONS

Axis I: V61.21   Sexual Abuse of Child
               V71.02   Adolescent Antisocial Behavior
               312.8x   Conduct Disorder
               _____   _____
               _____   _____

Axis II: V71.09   No Diagnosis on Axis II
               _____   _____
               _____   _____

CHRONIC PAIN

BEHAVIORAL DEFINITIONS

1. Suffers from daily pain sufficiently severe to impair functioning at work, home, and leisure pursuits.
2. Overuse or use of increased amounts of medications with little, if any, pain relief.
3. Complaints of generalized pain in many joints, muscles, and bones that debilitates normal functioning.
4. Experiences tension, migraine, cluster, or chronic daily headaches.
5. Experiences back or neck pain.
6. Consulted with or under the care of a medical practitioner who has failed to provide relief from the pain.
7. Limited ability to focus attention on anything independent of physical pain.
8. Feelings of isolation, loneliness, and frustration as the result of limitations on activities due to constant pain.
9. Feelings of despair about the potential for recovery.
10. Reduced decision-making effectiveness due to distraction of physical pain.

—. _____
   _____
—. _____
   _____
—. _____
   _____

LONG-TERM GOALS

1. Increase awareness of basic information about the most effective methods of controlling chronic pain.
2. Decrease level of physical pain being experienced by using non-medical adjunctive skills, including relaxation and other stress management techniques.
3. Reduce the disruption that chronic pain has caused in daily activities.
4. Set realistic goals, including returning to work either full- or part-time.
5. Increase ability to make new decisions based on the changes pain has wrought in daily life.
6. Accept a degree of chronic pain as unavoidable and build a life around it without resentment.

—. _____

_____

—. _____

_____

—. _____

_____

SHORT-TERM OBJECTIVES

1. Verbalize the nature of current painful condition that led to joining the group. (1)
2. Describe the history of physical condition and pain. (2)
3. Identify the feelings that chronic pain has generated. (3, 5)
4. List the impact that pain has had on work and personal life. (4, 5)
5. Verbalize an increased understanding that chronic

THERAPEUTIC INTERVENTIONS

1. Ask each member to describe his/her medical condition and the situation that precipitated joining the group.
2. Elicit from group members their history of pain, including treatments sought and diagnoses assigned.
3. Reinforce appropriate expression of feelings resulting from the condition of chronic pain (e.g., frustration, isolation, hopelessness, despair).

pain affects—and is affected by—the mind as well as the body. (6, 7)

6. Articulate the distinction between acute and chronic pain. (8, 9)

7. Verbalize an understanding of the physiology of pain. (10)

8. List some of the current medical treatment strategies for chronic pain and summarize personal experience with them. (11, 12)

9. Acknowledge the benefits of exercise in chronic pain control. (13)

10. Keep an exercise activity journal for a week. (14, 15)

11. Begin an exercise program of stretching and conditioning, working toward a goal of daily exercise. (16, 17)

12. Demonstrate deep abdominal breathing. (18)

13. Demonstrate progressive muscle relaxation. (19)

14. Demonstrate autogenic increased blood flow and healing imagery skills. (20, 21)

15. Demonstrate self-hypnosis skills using pain-control suggestions. (22)

16. Report a decrease in pain from using stress management techniques. (23, 24)

17. Identify negative cognitions that increase anxiety and stress, resulting in increased pain. (25, 26)

4. Encourage group members to share how their personal histories of pain have impacted their work and family relationships.

5. Facilitate group discussion about the emotional impact of chronic pain, using examples from speakers' personal experiences.

6. Encourage group discussion about the subjective nature of chronic pain: how people handle pain differently and how it can be influenced by family, environmental factors, cultural expectations, previous history, and possible compensations.

7. Provide additional information where necessary about the impact of chronic pain on emotional and intellectual functioning.

8. Teach group members the difference between *acute pain* (that resulting from a wound or broken bone, requiring immediate attention, and with a good prognosis for complete recovery) and *chronic pain* (persistent pain that remains long after an injury has recovered and can continue for months or years).

9. Elicit from group members personal examples that demonstrate their understanding of the distinction between acute and chronic pain.

18. Use thought-stopping techniques to escape from persistent negative thinking. (27)

19. Challenge negative cognitions using Ellis's ABCD model of cognitive restructuring. (28, 29)

20. Report reduced stress using stress inoculation techniques. (30, 31, 32)

21. List the secondary gain that chronic pain has provided. (33, 34)

22. Increase the use of assertive communication skills. (35, 36, 37)

23. Verbalize commitment to returning to work full- or part-time if at all possible. (38)

24. Develop a realistic plan for returning to work. (39, 40)

25. Identify sleep problems as they contribute to chronic pain. (41, 42)

26. Commit to a program aimed at maximizing sleep potential. (43)

27. Verbalize commitment to good nutrition as part of a general pain management program. (44)

28. Verbalize understanding of the many pain medications available, and evaluate realistic need for medication. (45)

29. Articulate long-term plan for coping with chronic pain. (46)

10. Teach group members some basic theories of chronic pain: the concept of pain "imprinting" (nervous system becomes conditioned to transmit particular pain messages); the role of pain receptors and neurotransmitters; and the gate-control theory, which hypothesizes that sufficient stimulation can shut down the pain response (e.g., rubbing a painful bump to reduce the pain).

11. Using group members' personal experiences, compile a list of current medical treatment strategies for chronic pain (e.g., electrical stimulation, acupuncture, trigger points, nerve blocks, heat and cold therapy, and massage).

12. Facilitate group discussion about members' experiences with these different treatment strategies.

13. Share with group members the research findings that exercise, in particular stretching and strengthening, can promote healing and reduce chronic pain.

14. Assign group members to keep a journal of their physical (exercise) activities for a week, including their attitudes toward exercise.

15. Review members' journals and facilitate group exploration of what members learned from monitoring

___. _____

   _____

___. _____

   _____

___. _____

   _____

their activities and attitudes.

16. Assist group members in
developing personal exer-
cise programs that include
a physician's approval, a
gradual building toward
daily exercise, and a combi-
nation of stretching and
conditioning exercises.

17. Periodically review members' progress toward incorporating exercise into their
daily routines.

18. Teach group members deep
abdominal breathing and
encourage daily practice.

19. Lead group members
through the progressive
muscle relaxation protocol,
where muscle groups are
first tensed and then re-
laxed.

20. Train group members in the
autogenic warming of their
hands and feet, resulting in
the benefits of healing due
to increased blood flow. Encourage members to practice
every day until mastery.

21. Lead group members
through four-step imagery
process: (1) deep relaxation;
(2) conjuring an image that
represents the chronic pain
(e.g., a hot branding iron
searing the body, a vice
gripping the head); (3) visualizing the healing process
that releases the pain (e.g.,
cool water washing away
the hot iron, the vice loosen-
ing and falling away); and

(d) visualizing self as happy, coping well, and growing stronger and healthier.

22. Assist group members in developing personal self-hypnosis induction tapes, incorporating steps for deepening a self-hypnotic trance, and going to a special peaceful place; suggest specific pain-reduction methods (e.g., directly reducing the pain sensation, changing the pain sensation to another sensation such as itchiness or tingling, relocating the pain sensation to a less incapacitating place such as the little finger, numbing the pain, or simply observing the pain without discomfort). Include posthypnotic suggestions to facilitate the benefits of the self-hypnosis.

23. Assign group members to practice at least one of the stress management or pain-reduction techniques (deep breathing, muscle relaxation, increased blood flow, healing imagery, self-hypnosis, etc.) at least once daily.

24. Review group members' experiences of using the stress management/pain-reduction techniques, reinforcing successes and gently confronting resistance.

25. Facilitate group discussion about how negative thinking has negative impact

(e.g., increased muscle tension, fatigue, depression) on the experience of chronic pain.

26. Help group members identify and monitor their own negative thoughts regarding their pain.

27. Teach thought-stopping techniques (snapping a rubber band worn around the wrist or mentally shouting "Stop" and then replacing negative thought with a hopeful, positive, realistic thought) and encourage members to practice regularly.

28. Describe to group members Ellis and Dryden's ABCD model of cognitive restructuring. A stands for the *activating* event (i.e., pain), B is own *belief* system or thoughts about the event, C represents the *consequences* of A and B (the resulting feelings), and D stands for *disputing* the negative thoughts or beliefs and replacing them with positive, realistic beliefs.

29. Assign members to practice cognitive restructuring and report back to the group on their experiences, reinforcing successes and redirecting failures.

30. Teach group members the stress inoculation technique of recognizing early signs of a strong emotional reaction and using specific coping

statements to relax and talk oneself through the pain (e.g., "Breathe deeply and relax," "I can cope with this, I've done it before," "This is just temporary, the pain never lasts more than an hour").

31. Assist group members in developing personal lists of specific coping statements to use when feeling a strong emotional reaction.

32. Assign group members to practice stress inoculation during the week and report back on their successes.

33. Facilitate group discussion about the concept of secondary gain (the compensations one derives from being in pain).

34. Help members identify personal experiences with secondary gain, including being taken care of, getting support, lowering expectations, and so forth. Explain to members that understanding how they sometimes use their pain may help them gain better control over the pain.

35. Facilitate group discussion about the difference between passive, aggressive, and assertive styles of communication, noting the impact of each on the experience of chronic pain.

36. Teach assertive communication skills, including active listening, problem solving,

and assertive anger expression.

37. Using role play and behavioral rehearsal, have group members practice assertive communication skills in the group. Assign members to practice the skills *in vivo*.

38. Describe to group members the benefits of a return to work in some capacity (improved self-esteem promotes better healing), and elicit verbal commitment to returning to work if possible.

39. Facilitate group clarification of members' job values, the aspects of their jobs they are able to achieve, and modifications they would like to make.

40. Help group members develop plans for returning to work, including contacting potential employers and assessing job retraining services.

41. Facilitate group explorations of the relationship between sleep patterns and chronic pain.

42. Describe to group members the factors that affect sleep quality, including dietary considerations (caffeine, nicotine, alcohol, the regularity of mealtimes, supplements such as melatonin, etc.), sleep habits (using one's bed for activities other than sleeping or sex, bedtime rituals, daytime naps),

environmental factors (noise, light, comfort issues, etc.), obsessional thinking, exercise, and relaxation.

43. Elicit from group members ideas for maximizing own sleep potential and a verbal commitment to pursue such ideas.

44. Facilitate group discussion about the relationship between chronic pain and nutrition, and encourage members to commit to following a plan of good nutrition.

45. Using members' personal knowledge and experience, facilitate discussion about the medications available for combating pain. Help members realistically evaluate their need for medication.

46. Encourage group members' development of long-term plans for coping with chronic pain. Emphasize the need for the inclusion of daily exercise, stress-reduction skills, cognitive restructuring, assertive communication skills, good sleep habits, and healthy nutrition.

—. _____

_____

—. _____

_____

—. _____

_____

DIAGNOSTIC SUGGESTIONS

Axis I:	307.89	Pain Disorder Associated With Both Psychological Factors and (Axis II Disorder)
	307.80	Pain Disorder Associated With Psychological Factors
	300.7	Hypochondriasis
	300.81	Somatization Disorder
	316	Personality Traits Affecting (Axis III Disorder)
	316	Maladaptive Health Behaviors Affecting (Axis III Disorder)
	316	Psychological Symptoms Affecting (Axis III Disorder)
	_____	_____
	_____	_____

CODEPENDENCE

BEHAVIORAL DEFINITIONS

1. Preoccupation and extreme dependence (emotionally, socially, and sometimes physically) on a person or object.
2. Difficulty expressing needs and desires.
3. Feelings of responsibility toward others' feelings, thoughts, needs, wants, choices, and well-being.
4. Compulsion to help others solve their problems and feelings of anger when help is not appreciated.
5. Tendency to try to control other people and the outcome of events.
6. Feels an attraction to needy people.
7. Pattern of either blaming others for problems that are the responsibility of self or blaming self for others' problems.
8. Difficulty accepting help from others.
9. Feelings of low self-esteem.

—. _____

_____

—. _____

_____

—. _____

_____

LONG-TERM GOALS

1. Understand and recognize codependent behavior and its negative impact on life.
2. Clarify and strengthen relationship and responsibility boundaries.
3. Develop the ability to identify and assertively express feelings, needs, and desires.

4. Take responsibility for own choices and stop expecting others to meet needs or desires.
5. Improve self-esteem and decrease feelings of worthlessness.
6. Develop appropriate self-nurturing behaviors and reduce caretaking behaviors toward others.
7. Decrease self-critical thoughts and statements.

—. _____

_____

—. _____

_____

—. _____

_____

SHORT-TERM OBJECTIVES

1. Verbalize an understanding of what codependent behavior is and its negative impact on life. (1, 2)
2. Verbalize an understanding of how codependence is based on low self-esteem and identify causes for low self-esteem in his/her life. (2, 3)
3. Describe own codependent behavior as it is experienced in daily life interactions. (1, 4, 5, 6)
4. Verbalize the difference between emotional needs and personal desires. (7)
5. Identify own emotional needs and personal desires. (8)
6. Practice the expression of own emotional needs and personal desires within the

THERAPEUTIC INTERVENTIONS

1. Elicit group members' perceptions of their own codependent behaviors.
2. Present additional material on codependence if necessary to supplement members' perceptions, and teach an accurate understanding of this pattern of behavior.
3. Encourage group discussion of the relationship between codependent behavior and low self-esteem, teaching how codependent behavior stems from low self-esteem and a severe need for acceptance. Ask each member to identify experiences from his/her life that have contributed to low self-esteem.
4. Describe the family-sculpting exercise.
5. Have each member develop a sculpture of a typical

group first and then in daily life circumstances. (9, 10, 11)

7. Identify own attempts to control others' behaviors. (12)

8. Describe situations that can reasonably be expected to be controlled and those that cannot be controlled. (13)

9. Identify fears associated with not being in control of situations. (14, 15)

10. Identify the childhood experiences that led to a need to control. (16)

11. Verbalize an understanding of the concept of compassionate detachment versus rejection. (17, 18, 19)

12. Report on the *in vivo* practice of compassionate detachment toward others' needs in order to reduce caretaking behavior. (20, 21, 22)

13. Define own personal rights. (23)

14. Verbalize an understanding of where own responsibility for satisfying others' emotional needs begins and ends. (24, 25)

15. State limits that will be set for helping others meet their needs and for accepting help from others for meeting own needs; develop consequences for noncompliance with those limits. (26, 27, 28)

16. Listen to another person describe his/her feelings and

scene of turmoil in their family, using other group members as role players. The active member positions each participating person and explains who he or she represents in the family.

6. After each sculpting exercise, process the group members' feelings arising from directing, role-playing, or witnessing the experience.

7. Clarify the differences between needs and desires.

8. Assist group members in identifying their emotional needs and personal desires.

9. Practice members' assertive expression of emotional needs and personal desires in small groups.

10. Assign group members to express emotional needs and personal desires during the week, including asking for help or support.

11. Process group members' success in attempting to assertively express their needs and desires.

12. Explore ways in which group members attempt to control others' behavior.

13. Elicit examples from group members of situations they have control over versus situations they do not have control over.

14. Explore members' feelings about the situations in which they do not have control.

needs without verbalizing responsibility for causing those feelings and for meeting those needs. (29, 30)

17. Practice using "I" statements to express feelings. (31, 32)

18. Communicate feelings honestly in the group and then to significant others outside of the group. (33, 34, 35)

19. Report a reduction in feelings of shame, fear, and resentment. (36)

20. Demonstrate congruity between thoughts/feelings and verbal and nonverbal communication. (37, 38)

21. Identify and implement self-nurturing behaviors. (39, 40)

22. Identify negative cognitions and replace them with reality-based, self-affirming cognitions. (41, 42)

—. _____
_____

—. _____
_____

—. _____
_____

15. Explore group members' fears of giving up attempts to be in control.

16. Facilitate group members' exploration of underlying feelings associated with not being in control and the childhood events that may be causally related to the need for control.

17. Teach the relationship between letting go of control and the concept of compassionate detachment (i.e., caring for another person but maintaining boundaries of responsibility for behavior and decisions).

18. Have group members discuss the distinction between detachment and rejection and relate it to their own lives.

19. Discuss with group members the concept of a higher power that runs the universe and how it helps with letting go of control. Encourage members to share their own ideas (or alternatives) of this concept.

20. In small groups, have members develop strategies for handling situations at home with detachment.

21. Assign group members to try using at least one of their detachment strategies during the week with significant others.

22. Have members report back to the group on their suc-

cess in applying detachment strategies during the week.

23. Elicit from group members a list of "personal rights."

24. Teach the differences between enmeshed relationships and those with healthy boundaries.

25. Have group members sculpt examples of enmeshed relationships and those with healthy boundaries.

26. Role-play verbally setting boundaries in the examples of enmeshed relationships that were sculpted.

27. Have each group member develop a limit-setting statement describing the situation, their feelings, and their desires for at least one situation where they need to protect their boundaries.

28. Help group members develop consequences for when others are noncompliant with the limits set.

29. Teach active listening skills.

30. In small groups, have members practice active listening skills rather than solution-finding responses; confront any inappropriate ownership of responsibility.

31. Teach the concept of "I" statements (e.g., "I feel _____ when you _____ because _____. I would like _____"), and have group members practice in small groups.

32. Discuss the idea that the expression of feelings is a healthy alternative to controlling or codependent behavior.

33. Encourage the expression of feelings in the group.

34. Facilitate the development of feeling statements for each group member about people they care about. Role-play the expression of these statements in small groups.

35. Assign group members to use at least one of their feeling statements during the week when they find themselves in a potential caretaking situation.

36. Teach how expressing feelings honestly and openly using "I" messages can deal appropriately with situations that stir up feelings of fear, shame, and resentment.

37. Ask each group member to give an example of behavior that was congruent with his/her feelings and thoughts and then an example in their recent experience when they behaved in an incongruent manner.

38. Demonstrate and encourage group members to empathically point out congruity and incongruity in any group members' behavior.

39. Elicit from group members examples of self-nurturing

behaviors (e.g., eating a favorite meal, taking a leisurely warm bath, viewing a movie of his/her choosing, going to a play or concert, having coffee or lunch with a friend) and obtain a commitment from each member to practice at least one of their examples each day.

40. Have members report back to the group their success with self-nurturing.

41. Explore with the group the cognitive messages that trigger feelings of worthlessness.

42. Facilitate the development of alternative, self-affirming cognitions.

__. _____
    _____

__. _____
    _____

__. _____
    _____

DIAGNOSTIC SUGGESTIONS

Axis I: 300.4   Dysthymic Disorder
              311   Depressive Disorder NOS

              ____   _____
              ____   _____

Axis II: 301.6   Dependent Personality Disorder

              ____   _____
              ____   _____

DEPRESSION

BEHAVIORAL DEFINITIONS

1. Feeling depressed or down nearly every day.
2. Decreased productivity on the job and in general.
3. Little pleasure in formerly pleasurable activities.
4. Withdrawal from social relationships.
5. Negative, dysfunctional cognitions.
6. Feelings of low self-esteem.
7. Feelings of hopelessness and helplessness possibly accompanied by suicidal thoughts.
8. Not actively suicidal.
9. Low levels of activity accompanied by feeling tired all the time.
10. Changes in sleep patterns.
11. Changes in appetite and eating habits.
12. Difficulty concentrating.
13. No underlying medical causes of the depression.
14. Not actively psychotic.

—. _____
_____

—. _____
_____
_____

—. _____
_____

LONG-TERM GOALS

1. Eliminate significant depressive symptoms and practice relapse prevention.

2. Replace negative, dysfunctional cognitions that precipitate depression with positive, health-enhancing cognitions that counteract depression.
3. Increase number of pleasant activities engaged in.
4. Improve feelings of self-esteem.
5. Increase productivity.
6. Reinvest in social relationships.

—. _____

_____

—. _____

_____

—. _____

_____

SHORT-TERM OBJECTIVES

1. State reason for attending group. (1)
2. Articulate identifying information about self apart from being depressed. (2)
3. Identify own symptoms of depression. (3)
4. Identify suicidal thoughts; state commitment to contact emergency resources if necessary. (4, 5, 8)
5. Verbalize realistic optimism about the group's ability to help conquer depression. (6)
6. Monitor and keep a chart of mood changes and contributing factors. (7, 9, 10)
7. Verbalize an understanding of the distinction between thoughts and feelings. (11, 12)

THERAPEUTIC INTERVENTIONS

1. Have members make a statement of purpose for participating in the group.
2. Have members introduce themselves to the rest of the group without reference to their depression.
3. Elicit group members' symptoms of their depression, including feelings, behaviors, and thoughts. Develop a list of common symptoms.
4. Ask members about occurrence of suicidal thoughts. Provide all group members with emergency resources (e.g., 24-hour crisis line or suicide-prevention line).
5. Ask members to state a commitment to contact emergency resources if necessary.

8. Verbalize an understanding of the ability of thoughts to influence feelings. (13, 14)

9. Identify thoughts that cause and maintain depressed feelings. (15, 16, 17)

10. Categorize thoughts that lead to depression. (18, 19, 20)

11. Demonstrate success at reducing negative thoughts that foster feelings of depression and anxiety. (21, 22)

12. Identify thoughts that lead to positive feelings. (23, 24, 25)

13. Demonstrate success using thoughts that improve mood. (26)

14. Verbalize understanding of the ABCD method of cognitive restructuring. (27, 28)

15. Verbalize examples of success using the ABCD model to modify errors in thinking. (29)

16. Verbalize understanding of the relationship between depressed thinking and low levels of pleasurable activity. (30, 31)

17. Identify activities that might be pleasurable. (32, 33, 34)

18. Predict anticipated pleasure of activities engaged in daily. (35)

19. Increase number of pleasurable activities engaged in daily. (35, 36, 37)

6. Explain the concept of cognitive behavioral therapy and describe research data that attests to the success of such therapy in combating depression.

7. Assign group members to complete the Beck Depression Inventory (BDI) or similar suicide risk assessment instrument on a weekly basis.

8. Regularly assess for suicidality. (See item #9 on BDI).

9. Assign members to monitor their moods to facilitate identification of factors that improve or worsen these moods. Use a 10-point scale, where 9 represents the best mood they can imagine, 0 the worst mood they can imagine, and 5 a typical mood when they are not depressed. Have members rate their mood each night before bed and keep a chart. If mood varies during the day, have members assign a best and worst score each day.

10. Confront members' assertions that they feel terrible all the time. Encourage monitoring of time of day and specific circumstances that might contribute to mood differences.

11. Clarify the distinction between thoughts (i.e., things people say to themselves about what goes on around

20. Implement a reward schedule for small increases in activity. (38)

21. Set clear, realistic goals to improve time management and planning. (39, 40)

22. Demonstrate success in time management and planning. (41)

23. Verbalize an understanding of the relationship between depressed thinking and social isolation. (42)

24. Initiate more pleasurable social activities. (43, 44, 45, 46, 47)

25. Monitor and report on the level and enjoyment of social activities. (47, 48)

26. Articulate the distinction between passive, aggressive, and assertive behavior. (49)

27. Express feelings, thoughts, and needs assertively and openly in group and later with significant others. (50, 51, 52, 53)

28. Practice enhanced communication skills. (54, 55)

__. _____
_____

__. _____
_____

__. _____
_____

them) and feelings (i.e., physiological responses in the body or mood states).

12. Facilitate group discussion about the influence on thoughts of family, culture, and individual personality traits.

13. Teach group members that the way thoughts influence feelings is by presenting a specific interpretation of events to the listener. The listener then reacts to that interpretation with a specific feeling.

14. Elicit members' descriptions of their thoughts influencing their feelings, and encourage members to relate their own experiences to those of the speaker.

15. Encourage members to pay attention to their thoughts on a regular basis, with particular focus on the recurring ones.

16. Teach group members to identify the thoughts that cause and maintain depression by working backward from feelings to thoughts (e.g., ask members to notice when they are feeling particularly bad, and then notice what they are saying to themselves at those times [thoughts]). Assign members to monitor this during the week.

17. Review members' insights from monitoring their

depression-causing or -maintaining thoughts.

18. Teach group members the major categories of distorted thinking (all-or-nothing thinking, "shoulds," labeling, filtering, overgeneralization, magnification, etc.).

19. Have members categorize their thoughts as they monitor them throughout the week and report back to the group the following week.

20. Teach the concepts of necessary versus unnecessary (worrying) thinking.

21. Encourage group members to try to decrease the incidence of unnecessary, distorted thinking using thought-stopping techniques (e.g., mentally shouting "Stop!" or snapping rubber band worn around the wrist) to interrupt negative thoughts.

22. Assign group members who identify themselves as "worriers" to set aside 15 to 30 minutes a day to worry, postponing until then worry thoughts that come up at other times.

23. Demonstrate the development of more-rational statements to replace the distortions.

24. Help group members develop a list of positive, mood-enhancing thoughts and affirmations that can

be read daily. Have members include statements that give credit for tasks accomplished each day.

25. Ask members to read their lists of positive thoughts and affirmations every day.

26. Review and reinforce members' success in improving their mood using their positive thoughts and affirmations.

27. Teach Ellis and Dryden's ABCD method of cognitive restructuring. (A is the *activating* event that precedes negative feelings; B is the distorted *belief* about that event that causes the negative feelings; C is the *consequences* of the belief or the negative feelings; and D is *disputing* the distorted belief with realistic, positive thoughts.)

28. Help individual group members demonstrate examples of the ABCD method. Help them identify the activating event, the belief about the event, the consequent negative feelings, and help them dispute that belief.

29. Assign group members to practice the ABCD method during the week and report their progress the following week, reinforcing successful implementation and redirecting unsuccessful attempts.

30. Facilitate group discussion about the cycle wherein de-

pression leads to decreased activity, which in turn increases depression.

31. Ask members to share their own experiences of this cycle with the rest of the group.

32. Elicit from group members activities (preferably ordinary, simple things like taking a walk, taking a bubble bath, watching a sunset) that they find—or used to find—pleasurable.

33. Give each member a copy of the *Pleasant Events Schedule* (MacPhillamy and Lewinsohn) to read to help increase ideas for potentially pleasurable activities. Have members share any insights gained from the list.

34. Assign group members to monitor daily participation in the pleasant events on their personal lists.

35. Assign group members to participate in a new activity from their pleasant-activity list in the next week. Ask them to predict ahead of time how much pleasure they will derive from the activity and to assess afterward how pleasurable the activity actually was.

36. Review members' progress, including the effect of pleasurable activities on mood.

37. Facilitate group discussion about how negative antici-

patory thoughts can interfere with motivation to participate in activities that can bring pleasure.

38. Have group members commit to rewarding themselves (e.g., eating a favorite meal, going to a movie, calling a friend) for engaging in a new activity, regardless of the outcome of the activity.

39. Ask group members to write a list of all the things they would like to accomplish the following week, including activities aimed at overcoming depression. Have them prioritize the items from A (top priority) to C (lowest priority).

40. Help members formulate goals that are clear, specific, and realistic, and ensure that there is a balance between instrumental and pleasurable activities.

41. Assign group members to use their plan during the week, reviewing and reinforcing their success the following week.

42. Elicit from members the negative consequences of the increasing isolation brought about by depression.

43. Facilitate group discussion about the benefits of a supportive social network.

44. Help group members generate a list of suggestions for meeting people and a list of

activities in which they could invite someone to join them.

45. Have group members role-play, in dyads, asking someone to join them in one of their pleasant activities.

46. Ask group members to initiate at least one social activity during the week.

47. Review and reinforce members' success in initiating social interaction.

48. Assign members to monitor their social interactions during the week, noting which were positive and which negative. Have members report back to the group the following week on their insights.

49. Clarify the distinction between passive, aggressive, and assertive behavior.

50. Teach assertive communication skills, including "I" statements.

51. Have group members role-play, in dyads, assertive responses to situations they are currently facing in their lives.

52. Assign members to practice assertive expression of feelings, thoughts, and desires to others during the week.

53. Have members share with the rest of the group their success in assertive communication, reinforcing success and redirecting failures.

54. Teach skills of communication effectiveness, including active listening skills, the importance of eye contact, and nonverbal communication.

55. Assign group members to practice communication skills in role plays, then with *in vivo* situations during the week.

___. _____

_____

___. _____

_____

___. _____

_____

DIAGNOSTIC SUGGESTIONS

Axis I:	296.2x	Major Depressive Disorder, Single Episode
	296.3x	Major Depressive Disorder, Recurrent
	300.4	Dysthymic Disorder
	311	Depressive Disorder NOS
	309.0	Adjustment Disorder With Depressed Mood
	_____	_____
	_____	_____
Axis II:	301.82	Avoidant Personality Disorder
	_____	_____
	_____	_____

DOMESTIC VIOLENCE OFFENDERS

BEHAVIORAL DEFINITIONS

1. Intentional infliction of physical pain or injury on partner; any action perceived by partner as having that intent (throwing objects at partner, pushing, grabbing, hitting, choking, etc.).
2. Intentional infliction of psychological pain or injury on partner; any action perceived by partner as having that intent (e.g., damaging partner's prized possessions, injury to pets, belittling or insulting partner, monitoring partner's whereabouts, restricting partner's access to friends).
3. Partner's fear of continuing physical injuries or emotional abuse resulting from assaultive acts, threats, intimidation, or berating by abusive partner.
4. Pattern of increasing frequency and severity of abusive episodes.
5. Periods of calm, loving ("honeymoon") behavior between abusive episodes.
6. Few communication or problem-solving skills.
7. Feelings of low self-esteem.
8. Expression of beliefs that support men's dominance over women.
9. Tendency to minimize, rationalize, or justify the violence.
10. Accepts at least some responsibility for abusive behavior.
11. No history of ritualized abuse, use of weapons, rape, or serious injury to partner.

—. _____
_____

—. _____
_____

—. _____
_____

LONG-TERM GOALS

1. Acknowledge and accept responsibility for own abusive behavior.
2. Eliminate all physical aggression in the relationship.
3. Eliminate all emotional abuse and coercion in the relationship.
4. Develop nonviolent alternatives for the expression of pain and anger in a relationship.
5. Increase ability to feel empathy for partner.

___. _____

_____

___. _____

_____

___. _____

_____

SHORT-TERM OBJECTIVES

1. Each member describes domestic violence that he perpetrated. (1, 2, 3)

2. Describe the emotional impact of listening to others talk about the pain they inflicted on a female partner. (4)

3. Practice using time-out to defuse a situation when anger-escalating behaviors begin. (5, 6, 7, 8)

4. Identify sensory, cognitive/emotional, and behavioral early warning signs of escalation toward violence. (9, 10)

5. Verbalize understanding of the cycle of violence. (11, 12)

6. Verbalize an understanding of the core beliefs that sus-

THERAPEUTIC INTERVENTIONS

1. Ask each group member to describe in detail the violent incidents that convinced him to participate in the group.

2. Facilitate group confrontation of any speaker's denial, minimizing, blaming, and female bashing.

3. Demonstrate and facilitate group support and approval for honesty and accountability.

4. Facilitate group discussion about the emotional impact of listening to each speaker's story.

5. Using role playing, modeling, and behavior rehearsal, teach the six components of time-out technique (*self-monitoring* for escalating

tain the pattern of violence. (13)

7. Articulate negative effects of violence on self, partner, and children. (14)

8. Identify vulnerable feelings and how they are transformed into anger. (15, 16, 20)

9. Practice identifying feelings of fear and sadness beneath anger. (17, 18, 20)

10. Express feelings and personal desires in an assertive feeling statement. (19, 20, 21)

11. Set specific, realistic, behavioral goals to achieve changes in relationship with partner, and report success in achieving these goals. (22, 23, 24)

12. Differentiate between statements that acknowledge responsibility and those that avoid responsibility. (2, 25)

13. Articulate a commitment to stop violent and controlling behaviors and to stop blaming partner for inciting abuse. (25, 26)

14. List the positive traits of masculinity. (27)

15. Demonstrate ability to listen empathically. (28, 29, 30)

16. Verbalize commitment to the lengthy process of repairing partner's trust. (31)

17. Identify abusive behaviors beyond those of physical violence. (32)

feelings of anger and hurt, *signaling* to partner that verbal engagement should end, *acknowledging* the need of partner to disengage, *separating* to disengage, *cooling down* to regain control of anger, and *returning* to controlled verbal engagement).

6. Facilitate discussion with group members about the use of time-out, and explore their resistance to using it.

7. Elicit group members' commitments to use time-outs whenever necessary during the week.

8. Review members' experiences with time-out during the week, redirecting unsuccessful and reinforcing successful implementation.

9. Solicit examples from group members of the warning signs that prompted use of time-out. Write these on a list in three categories: *sensory* (e.g., tension in chest or arms, increased heart rate or breathing), *thoughts* (e.g., "You dirty _____"; "This isn't fair"), and *actions* (e.g., shouting, pacing, getting quiet).

10. Lead members through a visualization of the incident that brought them to treatment. Ask them to identify what they were feeling emotionally and physiologically at different intervals before the violence, and discuss

18. Identify abusive childhood experiences and express feelings associated with those experiences. (33, 34)

19. Identify the influence of own parents' child-raising styles on violent behavior in current family. (35, 36)

20. Identify unmet emotional needs that fuel the behavior of controlling the partner. (37, 38, 39)

21. Verbalize an understanding of the way racism, sexism, and homophobia are linked to victimization. (40, 41)

22. Identify the cultural stereotypes that constrict sexual enjoyment for men and women and foster beliefs in male dominance. (42)

23. Make transition to couples therapy. (43)

___. _____
   _____

___. _____
   _____

___. _____
   _____

how they were behaving at those same intervals.

11. Teach group members the five steps in the cycle of violence: (1) *violent incident,* (2) *the honeymoon phase,* (3) *tension-building phase* (normal family conflicts), (4) *increasing anger,* (5) *escalation behavior* (verbal abuse, destruction of property, etc.), leading back to the violent incident. Stress that over time the cycles get shorter and more violent.

12. Encourage members to identify and share with the rest of the group their particular behaviors that correspond to the five different steps of the cycle of violence.

13. Describe some core beliefs that sustain men's patterns of violence (e.g., "I'm the boss of this household"; "I should be able to control her"); encourage group members to identify and articulate their own beliefs.

14. Facilitate group discussion of the negative effects of their violence on themselves, their partners, and their children.

15. Give members handouts listing adjectives to describe vulnerable feelings for use as a reference in identifying their own emotional experiences; ask each member to describe at least one incident of experiencing a vulnerable feeling.

16. Explain to group members the transition of vulnerable feelings (e.g., powerlessness, grief, loneliness, sadness, humiliation, hurt, shame, nervousness) to more powerful feelings (e.g., anger, rage).

17. Solicit examples from members of angry feelings, and explore the more vulnerable feelings underneath. As a starting point, focus in particular on the underlying sadness and fear.

18. Facilitate group discussion of the benefits and costs of experiencing and expressing more of their vulnerable feelings instead of anger and rage.

19. Teach group members the assertive feeling statement ("I feel _____ when you because I _____. I would like _____").

20. Help group members identify their feelings and practice expressing them in feeling statements.

21. Assign members to practice using feeling statements during the week and report on their success the following week.

22. Assign group members, in dyads, to formulate specific, realistic, behavioral goals toward reducing violence in their relationships. Provide assistance where needed.

23. Encourage dyads to explore the questions of what will

be gained and lost in achieving the set goals.

24. Review members' progress in meeting their goals, redirecting failures and reinforcing successes.

25. Solicit examples from group members of statements that reflect an acknowledgment of responsibility for violent behavior (e.g., "I hit her"; "I am in charge of my own actions"), versus those that avoid or deflect responsibility (e.g., "The next thing I knew, she was lying on the ground"; "She always provokes me").

26. Elicit verbal commitment from group members to stop violent and controlling behaviors and to stop blaming partners for inciting abuse.

27. Ask group members to brainstorm positive human qualities they would look for in a friend or partner. Then have members brainstorm what qualities it takes to be a man. Facilitate discussion about the contrast between the list that results from cultural pressure and the need to expand definitions of masculinity.

28. Teach group members the skill of empathic listening (e.g., eye contact, calm voice, reflection of speaker's feelings, no interruption).

29. Facilitate group exploration about how empathic listen-

ing might have helped during conflict escalations.

30. Have group members practice, in dyads, role-playing empathic listening in response to a provocative statement.

31. Facilitate group discussion of the fact that trust of a partner can be rebuilt only with time and a commitment to treat partner with respect, kindness, and compassion.

32. Using members' personal experiences, both as perpetrator and victim, list the many behaviors that are used in attempting to control another (e.g., the silent treatment, taking away the car keys, withholding child support). Explore members' feelings about the magnitude of the list.

33. Ask members, in dyads, to identify and explore a time when each man was a victim of violence and then a time during the same period when each man was himself violent.

34. Facilitate group discussion about the roots of violence and the potential effects of their own violence on their children.

35. Ask each group member to describe what he learned from his mother and father, respectively, about violence and about being a man. En-

courage appropriate expression of feelings.

36. Discuss with group members the impact of family-of-origin experiences on violent behavior in current family.

37. Teach group members that attempts to control the partner is a strategy for meeting one's own needs (e.g., need to feel important, powerful, effective, successful, masculine, recognized) when one feels unable to meet those needs oneself; assist members in identifying their unmet emotional needs.

38. Brainstorm with group members alternative ways of meeting own emotional needs, and assign members to use the alternatives during the week.

39. Review group members' success in using alternative strategies to meet their own emotional needs.

40. Explore with group members how the fear of victimization (because of being associated with a minority group) leads to oppression of that group and the creation of stereotypes.

41. Facilitate group discussion of homophobia, racism, and sexism, helping members identify their stereotypes, the ways they behave that maintain those stereotypes, and the ways in which they may have been hurt by each of these beliefs.

42. Using role plays, help group members identify the cultural stereotypes about men and women's sexual behavior (e.g., women don't really need sex as much as men, women should always be willing to fulfill men's desires, men should initiate sex, women shouldn't ask for what they want sexually). Facilitate discussion about how these stereotypes limit sexual enjoyment of both men and women and foster belief in male dominance and control.

43. Evaluate appropriateness of couples therapy for individual group members and make the appropriate referrals.

—. _____
   _____

—. _____
   _____

—. _____
   _____

DIAGNOSTIC SUGGESTIONS

Axis I:	V61.1	Physical Abuse of Adult
	312.43	Intermittent Explosive Disorder
	_____	_____
	_____	_____
Axis II:	301.7	Antisocial Personality Disorder
	301.83	Borderline Personality Disorder
	301.81	Narcissistic Personality Disorder
	_____	_____
	_____	_____

DOMESTIC VIOLENCE SURVIVORS

BEHAVIORAL DEFINITIONS

1. Self-report of intentional infliction of physical pain or injury by partner; any action perceived as having that intent (e.g., having objects thrown at self, being pushed, grabbed, hit, choked).
2. Intentional infliction of psychological pain or injury by partner; any action perceived as having that intent (e.g., having one's prized possessions damaged, injury to one's pets, being belittled or insulted, having one's whereabouts monitored, having one's access to friends restricted).
3. Fear of continuing physical injury or emotional abuse resulting from partner's assaultive acts, threats, intimidation, or berating.
4. Pattern of increasing frequency and severity of abusive episodes.
5. Periods of calm, loving ("honeymoon") behavior between abusive episodes.
6. A lack of communication or problem-solving skills.
7. Feelings of helplessness and hopelessness about own and children's safety.
8. Feelings of low self-esteem.
9. Tendency to minimize, rationalize, or justify the violence.

—. _____
   _____

—. _____
   _____

—. _____
   _____

LONG-TERM GOALS

1. Establish safety plans for self and children (i.e., concrete plan detailing cues for danger and steps that will be taken to ensure safety).
2. Examine pros and cons of remaining in the relationship.
3. Increase feelings of autonomy and self-esteem.
4. Develop necessary support system for surviving alone, if appropriate.
5. Develop behavioral repertoire for derailing cycle of violence, if appropriate.

—. _____
   _____

—. _____
   _____

—. _____
   _____

SHORT-TERM OBJECTIVES

1. Each group member introduce herself and state the abusive incident that precipitated joining the group. (1, 2, 3)
2. Verbalize acceptance of the ground rules of the group. (4)
3. Tell personal story of relationship violence. (2, 3, 5)
4. Describe current situation with respect to issues of safety for self and children. (6, 7)
5. Identify behaviors that typically signal the escalation toward violence. (8, 9)
6. Develop plan for escape if violence erupts or becomes imminent. (10)

THERAPEUTIC INTERVENTIONS

1. Ask each member to introduce herself and describe the abusive incident that precipitated joining the group.
2. Facilitate confrontation of any speaker's minimization, denial, or rationalization of her partner's violence.
3. Demonstrate and facilitate the group's empathic support to the speaker describing her painful experiences.
4. Explain and ask for a commitment to the ground rules, with special regard to maintaining confidentiality of each others' whereabouts to partners.

7. Verbalize understanding of the cycle of violence and identify behavioral examples from own experience. (11, 12)

8. Identify and express feelings connected to the relationship violence. (13)

9. Articulate negative effects of violence on self and children. (14)

10. List fears associated with leaving the relationship and reasons each feared result is likely or unlikely to materialize. (15, 16)

11. List possible outcomes of staying in the relationship. (17, 18)

12. Report on the objective evidence for partner showing sincere remorse for violence. (19)

13. Evaluate pros and cons of remaining in the relationship. (20)

14. Decrease statements of, and reported feelings of, self-blame for the violence, putting responsibility solely on the perpetrator. (2, 21, 22)

15. Give phone number to other group members and agree to call and to accept calls as a means of mutual support. (23)

16. Verbalize decrease in shameful feelings. (21, 22, 24)

17. If appropriate, practice time-out to defuse a situation when anger-escalating

5. Elicit from group members their personal stories of domestic violence, including triggers, frequency, and severity of violent incidents, whether the law has been involved, and whether their partners are involved in treatment to prevent continued abuse.

6. Have group members describe their current living arrangements (e.g., at home with abusive partner, apart from partner, with friend, in a shelter) and help them evaluate their safety and the safety of their children.

7. Supply information about shelters and 24-hour hot lines if necessary.

8. Explore with group members their own and their partners' behaviors that typically signal the escalation of violence (increase in loudness of voice, name-calling, threats, breaking things, etc.).

9. Facilitate group discussion of the emotions that often precede anger (hurt, fear, guilt, etc.) and of the cognitions associated with those emotions that trigger anger (e.g., He thinks I'm a jerk," He's going to leave me, "I've messed up again").

10. Help group members develop a plan for escaping their partners' violence or potential violence (e.g., packing a bag with money,

behaviors begin.
(19, 25, 26, 27)

18. Differentiate between contributing to conflict versus
contributing to violence in a
relationship. (28)

19. Verbalize acceptance of responsibility for conflict in
the relationship. (29)

20. Identify weak links in the
abusive chain where a new
constructive behavior could
most easily be substituted
for the old, dysfunctional,
negative interaction. (30, 31)

21. Verbalize increased awareness of needs and choices.
(32, 33)

22. Identify childhood experiences that contributed to an
acceptance or tolerance of
abusive behavior in a relationship. (34, 35)

23. Identify distorted self-
critical cognitions. (9, 36)

24. Identify and implement
reality-based, self-affirming
cognitions to replace critical
self-talk. (37, 38)

25. Identify mistaken beliefs
that fuel critical cognitions.
(39)

26. Report success in countering
mistaken beliefs using Socratic questions and positive
affirmations. (40, 41, 42)

27. Express feelings, including
anger, openly and honestly
in group. (43, 44, 47)

28. Articulate difference between passive (including

car keys, important docu-
ments, clothes, and toys and
storing it at a friend's;
knowing ahead of time
where they will go to avoid
being easily found; clarifying an escape route from
the house).

11. Teach group members the
five steps in the cycle of violence: (1) *violent incident,*
(2) *the honeymoon phase,*
(3) *tension-building phase*
(normal family conflicts),
(4) *increasing anger,* (5) *escalation behavior* (verbal
abuse, destruction of property, etc.) leading back to
the violent incident. Stress
that over time the cycles get
shorter and more violent.

12. Encourage members to
identify and share with the
rest of the group their own
and their partner's behaviors that correspond to the
five different steps of the
cycle of violence.

13. Elicit from group members
their complex feelings, including guilt and shame, associated with the domestic
violence.

14. Facilitate group discussion
of the negative effects of violence on their lives and
those of their children (e.g.,
living with a constant uncertainty and fear of harm,
children exposed to a model
of violence, feelings of
shame and low self-esteem).

passive-aggressive), aggressive, and assertive behaviors. (45)

29. Demonstrate assertiveness skills, including those needed to negotiate personal needs and desires. (46)

30. Increase implementation of daily self-nurturing behaviors. (48, 49)

31. Identify own violent behavior with children and comply with appropriate referral to a parenting group. (50)

—. _____
   _____

—. _____
   _____

—. _____
   _____

15. Assign group members to list fears associated with leaving the relationship (e.g., being alone, being unable to support oneself and one's children financially, being unable to make friends, being killed by abandoned partner, losing partner's love); have members describe why each feared result is likely or unlikely to happen.

16. Facilitate group sharing of members' fears of leaving their relationships.

17. Assign group members to list the possible outcomes of staying in the relationship (e.g., negative emotional and/or physical impact on children, negative impact on own self-esteem, possibility of severe physical injury or death, limited access to friends, family, and social activities).

18. Facilitate group sharing of possible outcomes of members staying in their relationships.

19. Teach group members the importance of partner experiencing remorse as a diagnostic tool in evaluating the chances of relationship changes versus partner using violence instrumentally without regret. Help members make the determination with respect to their own relationship.

20. Using the member-generated lists of fears of leaving and potential outcomes of staying, facilitate group discussion of the pros and cons of staying with a batterer.

21. Explore with group members the concept that violence in a relationship is solely the responsibility of the perpetrator.

22. Reinforce the concept of holding their abusive partners responsible for their decision to behave abusively when angry or wanting to control.

23. Foster members' support for each other by distributing, after permission has been privately obtained, a list of the names and phone numbers of all members. Encourage members to call each other between sessions.

24. Assign members to read material on domestic violence (e.g., *Battered Wives* by Martin, "Spouse Abuse" in *When Anger Hurts* by McKay, Rogers, and McKay) and discuss in the group.

25. Using role playing, modeling, and behavioral rehearsal, teach the six components of time-out technique: *monitoring* self for feelings of fear and partner for signals of escalating feelings of hurt and anger; *signaling* to partner that verbal engagement should

end; seeking *acknowledg-
ment* from partner of need
to disengage; *separating* to
disengage; *cooling down* to
diffuse conflict; and *returning* to controlled verbal engagement.

26. With safety as a primary
    consideration, encourage
    group members to use time-
    out only with those partners
    who have acknowledged
    their problem with anger
    and have committed to
    change. Remind members of
    their escape plans if time-
    out fails.

27. Review members' experi-
    ences using time-out with
    partners.

28. Help group members clarify
    the distinction between con-
    tributing to relationship
    conflict and deciding to be-
    have violently, noting that
    being responsible for the
    former does not mean one is
    responsible for the latter.

29. Elicit group members' ex-
    amples of ways in which
    they contribute to the con-
    flict in their relationships.

30. Teach group members how
    each negative interaction
    in a relationship conflict
    becomes a link in an abu-
    sive chain that results in
    violence.

31. Help group members iden-
    tify links in a typical abu-
    sive chain where they could
    substitute a new construc-
    tive behavior (e.g., active

listening, assertive feeling statement) for the negative interaction (e.g., blaming, belittling). Encourage group sharing of personal examples of these weak links.

32. Discuss with group members how coping with a violent partner can lead to a restricted awareness of own needs and desires, as well as an inaccurately limited perception of choices of how to behave at any given moment. Assign group members to monitor during the week their needs and personal desires, coupled with situations in which they felt they had limited choice in how to react.

33. Facilitate group discussion of members' experiences monitoring needs, desires, and perceived choices. Explore the idea of real versus perceived choices.

34. Elicit from group members examples of childhood and family experiences of violence or abuse.

35. Explore with group members the beliefs resulting from their childhood experiences that sustain tolerance for or acceptance of abusive behavior in a relationship.

36. Help group members identify the distorted, negative, and self-critical cognitions that trigger feelings of low self-esteem.

37. Assist group members in developing realistic, self-affirming cognitions to replace negative self-talk, and encourage members to practice during the week.

38. Review members' experiences in replacing negative cognitions, reinforcing successes and redirecting unsuccessful attempts.

39. Help members identify the mistaken beliefs resulting from childhood experiences that fuel self-critical cognitions and sustain acceptance or tolerance of abusive behavior in a relationship (e.g., "I don't deserve to be happy"; "It's okay for a man to beat his wife if she disobeys him").

40. Challenge members' beliefs using the Socratic method of questioning, and help them develop affirmations to counter the mistaken beliefs (e.g., "I deserve to be respected even if he disagrees with me about an issue"; "Women have equal rights to have opinions and make decisions").

41. Assign group members to practice *in vivo* challenging of their negative cognitions and mistaken beliefs.

42. Review members' experiences with cognitive restructuring, reinforcing success and redirecting failed attempts.

43. Explore with group members their fears about expressing anger, including the very real danger of eliciting their partners' violent reactions.

44. Help members write out their angry feelings before communicating them to another person.

45. Clarify the distinction between passive, passive-aggressive, aggressive, and assertive behavior.

46. Teach group members active listening skills and the use of assertive feeling statements ("I feel _____ when you _____ because I _____. I would like _____"). Then role-play situations where members make assertive requests of their dyad partners. Explore with group members the risks of using assertive behavior with their abusive partners.

47. Distribute a handout that lists many adjectives describing various emotions and then help group members identify their commonly experienced feelings and practice expressing them within the group.

48. Help members develop a list of self-nurturing behaviors (taking a bath, listening to music, going to a movie, reading a book, etc.) and assign daily completion of at least one item from the list.

49. Have members report to the group their success in self-nurturing.

50. Evaluate group members' own violent behaviors with children, and make appropriate referral to parenting group; assess the need to report the violence to a state child-welfare agency for protection of the children.

__. _____

_____

__. _____

_____

__. _____

_____

DIAGNOSTIC SUGGESTIONS

Axis I: 995.81   Physical Abuse of Adult, Victim
309.0   Adjustment Disorder With Depressed Mood
309.24   Adjustment Disorder With Anxiety
309.28   Adjustment Disorder With Mixed Anxiety and Depressed Mood
300.4   Dysthymic Disorder
296.xx   Major Depressive Disorder
309.81   Posttraumatic Stress Disorder

_____   _____

_____   _____

Axis II: 301.6   Dependent Personality Disorder

_____   _____

_____   _____

GRIEF/LOSS UNRESOLVED

BEHAVIORAL DEFINITIONS

1. Experience of the death of a loved person (parent, spouse, child, close friend).
2. Losses (divorce, job termination, child leaving home) that significantly impact daily life.
3. Feelings of sadness, problems with insomnia, weight loss, and other symptoms of depression resulting from the loss.
4. Shock, disbelief, numbness, and confusion as part of the grief reaction.
5. Difficulty focusing thoughts on anything but the loss.
6. Feelings of guilt for being alive and not having done enough for (or not saving) the lost significant other.
7. Guilt and shame over past misconduct, both real and imagined, that caused pain to the deceased.
8. Conflict between parents over how each grieves the loss of a child.
9. Avoidance of talking, except superficially, about the loss.
10. Lack of interest in or willingness to participate in social or recreational activities that might bring (or once might have brought) pleasure.

—. _____
_____

—. _____
_____

—. _____
_____

LONG-TERM GOALS

1. Begin and sustain a healthy emotional grieving process around the loss.
2. Develop awareness of how the avoidance of grieving and the attempts to deny the loss have affected life.
3. Complete the process of letting go of the lost significant other and the intense preoccupation with that loss.
4. Accept the permanence of the loss and begin renewing old relationships, initiating contacts with others, and participating in pleasurable activities.
5. Resolve feelings of guilt associated with the loss of the loved one.
6. Gradually but steadily return to level of functioning that was normal previous to the loss.
7. Develop control over emotional lability such that tearfulness is brief and less frequent or overwhelming.
8. Resolve conflict with significant others over differing grief reactions.

—. _____
   _____

—. _____
   _____

—. _____
   _____

SHORT-TERM OBJECTIVES

1. Verbalize the personal loss that led to joining the group. (1)
2. Share the story of the loss, including who was lost, when, and how the loss occurred. (2, 6)
3. Describe the impact of that loss on work, family, and relationships. (4, 6)
4. Begin expressing the feelings associated with the described losses. (3, 5, 6)

THERAPEUTIC INTERVENTIONS

1. Ask each group member to briefly describe the loss he/she experienced that precipitated joining the group.
2. Elicit from group members the full stories of their losses, including a description of the significant person and the circumstances of their loss.
3. Reinforce appropriate expression of speaker's feel-

5. Demonstrate the ability to give and accept empathic support. (6)

6. Verbalize an increased understanding of the components of grief as parts of a process that must be experienced in order to heal. (7, 8, 9)

7. Identify own position in the grieving process and describe personal experiences that confirm that position. (10)

8. Identify personal coping strategies, including the use of substances, and note those that may have interfered with the grieving process. (11)

9. Accept the need for antidepressant medication and follow through on a referral to a physician for an evaluation. (12)

10. Demonstrate ability to ask for help in group and with significant others. (13, 14)

11. Write a letter to the deceased person saying goodbye and expressing all the feelings experienced in the aftermath of the loss. (15, 16)

12. Verbalize the impact of the changed identity resulting from the loss. (17)

13. Articulate a realistic picture of the lost person—both positive and negative—and of the relationship with that person, and identify ways of

ings associated with the loss.

4. Encourage group members to share the impact of their personal loss on their ability to function at work, the rest of their family, and their relationships.

5. Elicit from group members a description of the range of feelings experienced since the loss and the ways members have attempted to cope with those feelings.

6. Offer, and facilitate other members offering, empathic support to speaker.

7. Teach group members that grief is a process rather than a stable thing, and describe the stages that most people experience: *shock* (including disbelief and numbness), *disorganization* (anger, powerlessness, guilt, fear, anxiety, sadness, despair, confusion, and disorientation), and *reorganization* (taking action, meeting challenges, coping with fears, releasing sadness, changing values, acceptance). (See *Beyond Grief* by Staudacher.)

8. Facilitate group discussion about the different stages of grief, highlighting how the stages neither follow any rigid order nor are independent from each other.

9. Stress to group members that healing can occur only if the process is not avoided but fully experienced.

remembering his/her special qualities. (18, 19, 20)

14. Report an increase in self-nurturing activities. (21, 22)

15. Develop a plan or ceremony to facilitate memorializing the lost person. (23, 24)

16. Verbalize self-care plans to cope with anniversary reactions. (25, 26)

17. Read books on the grief process and discuss their impact. (27)

18. Verbalize acceptance of the unique style of grieving of others close to the deceased. (28, 29)

19. Identify those who are being blamed for the loss of the loved one. (30)

20. Verbalize the desire to and beginning of the process of letting go of bitter blame for the loss of significant other. (31, 32)

21. Verbalize resolution of feelings of guilt or regret over actions toward lost loved one. (33)

—. _____
   _____

—. _____
   _____

—. _____
   _____

10. Encourage members to share personal experiences of the different stages of the grieving process. Assist them in identifying their position in the process.

11. Elicit from group members personal coping strategies for dealing with the pain of the loss (e.g., keeping a rigid schedule, limiting decision making, sleeping, asking for help, avoiding thinking or talking about the loss, increasing the use or abuse of substances). Encourage discussion of how some of the strategies may interfere with the grieving process (e.g., using substances prevents the experience of the feelings and thus slows healing).

12. Help members, where necessary, evaluate their need for antidepressant or other medication, and make the appropriate referrals.

13. Encourage group members to ask each other for emotional support (a gentle touch, a hug, a few minutes to describe their feelings, etc.).

14. Assist members in identifying sources of emotional support within their social network. Then assign members to ask for emotional support during the week from a significant person in their lives and to report back to the group on their experience.

15. Assign members to write a letter to the lost person expressing all the turmoil they have been experiencing since the loss and culminating in an expression of farewell.

16. Review members' experiences writing their farewell letters, providing empathic, emotional support where necessary.

17. Facilitate group discussion about the change in identity resulting from the loss (e.g., from being part of a married couple to being a widow, from being parent of a child to being a parent who has lost a child) and the impact of that identity change (e.g., the loss of respect, the loss of a role, the loss of self-esteem).

18. Elicit from group members stories about their lost significant person that highlight that person's positive characteristics. Have them bring photographs and other mementos to facilitate the storytelling.

19. Elicit from group members stories about their lost significant person that highlight that person's negative characteristics in order to present a realistic, balanced perspective.

20. Facilitate group discussion about the experience of recognizing both the positive and negative aspects of

their relationship with their lost person.

21. Have group members compile a personal list of self-nurturing behaviors (e.g., going for a walk, calling a friend, listening to music) and commit to completing at least two of those behaviors per day.

22. Review members' experiences of nurturing themselves, reinforcing successful experiences and gently confronting resistance.

23. Help members develop a plan or ceremony to memorialize their loved one (e.g., gather photographs and other mementos of the loved one and say a special goodbye; write a memorial letter of farewell to the loved one and go to a special place to read it; gather with friends or family and share reminiscences), and encourage members to carry out the plan or ceremony during the week or in the next session.

24. Facilitate members' memorializing ceremonies where appropriate, and encourage other members to describe the ceremonies held outside the group. Review the impact of these ceremonies on group members.

25. With members' permission, provide list of members' names, phone numbers, and the names and special dates

of their lost loved ones (e.g., birthdays, anniversaries). Encourage members to call each other on those days.

26. Have members develop personal self-care plans (good nutrition, adequate rest, contact with friends and family members, etc.) to facilitate the continuing process of grieving and the anticipated anniversary reactions.

27. Recommend that members read books on grief (e.g., *Getting to the Other Side of Grief: Overcoming the Loss of a Spouse* by Zonnebelt-Smeenge and DeVries, *The Bereaved Parent* by Schiff, *After the Death of a Child* by Finkbeiner) and process key ideas in the group.

28. Teach that grief is a very personal experience that varies greatly in its impact and how people cope with it.

29. Ask members to identify how other people close to the deceased have reacted to the loss, encouraging a nonjudgmental attitude of others' grieving styles.

30. Explore whether any members are blaming someone (e.g., self, spouse, doctors, perpetrator) for the death of the loved one.

31. Facilitate group feedback regarding the reasonableness of blaming someone for the death of the significant other.

32. If assigning responsibility seems reasonable, discuss the concept of forgiveness as a means of promoting healing rather than holding onto blame to promote alienation, bitterness, and anger. Recommend books such as *Forgive and Forget* (Smedes).

33. Use an empty-chair technique to say things to the deceased that were left unsaid or to ask for forgiveness for actions regretted; process the feelings within the group.

—. _____
    _____

—. _____
    _____

—. _____
    _____

DIAGNOSTIC SUGGESTIONS

Axis I: 296.2x   Major Depressive Disorder, Single Episode
            296.3x   Major Depressive Disorder, Recurrent
            309.0   Adjustment Disorder With Depressed Mood
            V62.82   Bereavement

            ____   _____
            ____   _____

Axis II: 301.6   Dependent Personality Disorder

            ____   _____
            ____   _____

HIV/AIDS

BEHAVIORAL DEFINITIONS

1. A positive diagnosis of HIV infection.
2. One or more of the AIDS-defining opportunistic infections (e.g., Kaposi's sarcoma, CMV, Pneumocystis pneumonia).
3. A diagnosis of AIDS.
4. Engaged in unsafe sexual practices that permitted the transmission of HIV from an infected partner.
5. Used a syringe for drug abuse that had previously been used by an HIV-infected person.
6. Received tainted blood during a blood transfusion, leading to HIV infection.
7. Feelings of guilt, shame, and anger over the behavior or circumstances that led to the HIV infection.
8. Shock, disbelief, numbness, fear, and confusion as part of the grief reaction to a diagnosis of HIV infection.
9. Feelings of guilt for being alive when so many friends have died from AIDS.
10. Experiences of prejudice and rejection among family, friends, and work colleagues for being HIV positive.

—. _____
_____

—. _____
_____

—. _____
_____

LONG-TERM GOALS

1. Begin and sustain a healthy emotional grieving process around the losses and limitations associated with HIV infection.
2. Resolve feelings of guilt and shame associated with the HIV infection.
3. Increase awareness of current treatment strategies for different symptoms of HIV infection.
4. Increase ability to make new decisions based on the changes wrought by HIV infection.
5. Make contingency plans for future care should the situation change or illness progress.
6. Reduce feelings of fear, anger, helplessness, and isolation.
7. Reach a state of acceptance of HIV status and build a life around it without resentment.

—. _____

_____

—. _____

_____

—. _____

_____

SHORT-TERM OBJECTIVES

1. Verbalize the current health condition that led to joining the group. (1)

2. Describe the history of HIV infection from diagnosis to present, including information about contraction of the virus and current treatment strategies. (2)

3. Report compliance with all physician-recommended tests, medications, and treatments. (3)

4. Demonstrate responsibility by adhering to the pre-

THERAPEUTIC INTERVENTIONS

1. Ask each group member to describe his/her current medical status, including HIV symptoms and limitations, and the precipitating reasons for joining the group.

2. Elicit from group members their history of HIV infection, including how the virus was contracted, diagnosis and the development of symptoms, and current medications and treatments recommended by personal physicians.

scribed schedule and conditions of medication ingestion. (4)

5. Report any medication side effects or symptoms experienced to physician or therapist. (5)

6. Express the feelings associated with being HIV positive/having AIDS. (6)

7. Demonstrate the ability to give and accept empathic support. (7)

8. Describe the impact that HIV infection has had on work and personal life. (8, 9)

9. Describe the history of previous losses associated with AIDS. (7, 10, 11)

10. Verbalize the stages of grief that must be experienced in order to remain emotionally healthy. (12, 13)

11. Identify own position in the process of grieving multiple deaths of close friends and lover and own anticipatory grief. (14, 15)

12. Identify suicidal ideas, intents, or plans associated with depression. (16)

13. Accept the need, where relevant, for antidepressant medication and follow through with a referral to a physician. (17)

14. Verbalize personal meaning of death and dying. (18, 19)

15. Identify own coping strategies, and verbalize more-adaptive strategies. (20, 21)

3. Probe members' compliance with physician's recommendations, including the consistent, timely taking of medications.

4. Explore reasons for medication noncompliance, and demonstrate and facilitate group members' confrontation of speaker's noncompliance.

5. Encourage group members to report any symptoms or medication side effects to physician or therapist.

6. Elicit and reinforce appropriate expression of feelings resulting from the diagnosis of and ongoing infection with the AIDS virus (e.g., anger, shame, isolation, helplessness, despair).

7. Offer, and facilitate other members offering, empathic support to speaker.

8. Encourage group members to share the impact of their AIDS/HIV infection on their work and personal lives.

9. Facilitate group discussion about the difficulties associated with maintaining romantic relationships in the face of fear of rejection, fear of infecting others, reluctance to reveal HIV status, and difficulties negotiating for safe sex.

10. Elicit from group members the multiple personal losses already experienced—or currently being suffered—

16. Evaluate own risk-taking behavior and consider the ramifications of continuing such behavior. (22, 23, 24)

17. Develop reinforcement strategies for maintaining low-risk behaviors. (25, 26, 27)

18. Describe own experiences with prejudice and discrimination over HIV status. (7, 28)

19. Verbalize experiences that result from the cultural attitudes surrounding HIV infection. (29, 30)

20. Describe own experiences with societal—and internalized—homophobia. (31, 32)

21. Acknowledge current substance use and list the ways it can make a negative impact on behavior control, judgment, and body chemistry. (33)

22. Follow through with a referral to a chemical-dependency treatment program. (34)

23. Practice safer IV drug-use strategies. (35)

24. Express feelings associated with the increasing dependence resulting from prolonged HIV infection. (7, 36)

25. Demonstrate increased use of strategies aimed at increasing own feelings of empowerment. (37, 38)

26. Identify social and community support systems. (39)

from AIDS, including friends, lovers, and family members.

11. Probe how these multiple previous losses affect members' reactions to their own diagnoses of AIDS/HIV infection.

12. Teach group members that grief is a process rather than a stable thing, and describe the stages that most people experience: *shock* (including disbelief and numbness), *disorganization* (including anger, helplessness, guilt, fear, anxiety, sadness, despair, confusion, and disorientation) and *reorganization* (including taking action, meeting challenges, coping with fears, releasing sadness, changing values, and acceptance). (See *Beyond Grief* by Staudacher.)

13. Facilitate group discussion about the different stages of grief, highlighting how the stages neither follow any rigid order nor are independent from each other. Discuss how each new crisis (HIV-positive diagnosis, development of symptoms, AIDS diagnosis, development of visible symptoms, etc.) can trigger a new bout of grief.

14. Using personal examples, help members identify their positions in the process of grieving for both their loved ones and themselves.

27. Exchange information about recent advances in treatment strategies or current experimental protocols available. (40)

28. Share strategies for obtaining concrete medical and social services. (38, 41, 42)

29. Demonstrate ability to ask for help in group and with significant others. (43, 44)

30. Verbalize self-care plans contingent on the progress of the infection. (45)

31. Verbalize contingency plans for own children in case of inability to care for them. (46)

32. Express feelings associated with "long-term-survivor" status. (47)

33. Articulate the impact of long-term-survivor status on career plans. (48)

34. List realistic, short-term goals to respond adaptively to HIV status. (49)

35. Commit to an ongoing program of good nutrition and general self-care. (50)

—. _____
_____

—. _____
_____

—. _____
_____

15. Facilitate group discussion about how the experience of multiple losses interferes with the grieving process. For example, the loss of so many friends in rapid succession along with the realistic anticipation of many more in the future can be overwhelming and make the transition from disorganization to reorganization difficult; survivor guilt in the face of so many losses can be a complicating factor.

16. Evaluate group members for suicidal ideas, intents, and plans associated with depression from grief over multiple losses, from the effects of HIV infection on appetite, sleep, and energy, and from the medication side effects versus plans that accompany a terminal illness and that demonstrate an attempt to maintain control over one's life/death.

17. Help members, where necessary, evaluate their need for antidepressant or antianxiety medication, and make the appropriate referrals.

18. Have group members share their feelings about the meaning of death and of dying from AIDS. Encourage members to share their spiritual beliefs about the after-death experience.

19. Probe group members for the belief that contracting the AIDS virus is retribution for unacceptable behavior (including being gay). Gently confront this belief.

20. Elicit from group members personal coping strategies (e.g., minimizing or reframing their condition, withdrawal and isolation, becoming more spiritually involved, substance use, and attempts to reconnect with family).

21. Facilitate group discussion about the adaptive nature of each strategy, and encourage the sharing, where appropriate, of more-adaptive strategies.

22. Assist group members in making an honest appraisal of their current high-risk behaviors (e.g., IV drug use, unsafe sex practices) related to the AIDS virus.

23. Facilitate group discussion about the conditions under which one might continue to engage in such behavior (such as, "If I'm HIV positive anyway, why bother?," substance use, and psychological denial).

24. Facilitate group discussion of the ramifications of continuing high-risk behaviors.

25. Help group members develop strategies for reinforcing and maintaining safer

sex practices (e.g., avoiding activities likely to trigger loneliness, such as going alone to a bar; the development of honest communication and assertive skills for negotiating condom use and other safe-sex practices; cognitive challenging of unhealthy justifications for unsafe sex; reduction of substance use; confronting internalized homophobia).

26. Assign group members to practice personal strategies for maintaining safe sex *in vivo*.

27. Periodically review members' experiences practicing safer sex, reinforcing successes and firmly confronting unsuccessful attempts.

28. Elicit group members' personal stories of rejection, prejudice, and discrimination since others have known of their HIV-positive status.

29. Facilitate group discussion about the personal/cultural factors contributing to the struggle with AIDS/HIV-positive status, including the stigmas, marginalization, sense of personal defectiveness, and disenfranchisement already experienced by minority groups (including gay and lesbian groups) long before the AIDS epidemic.

30. Elicit personal examples from group members to illustrate the cultural factors involved in the AIDS experience.

31. Encourage group sharing of members' experiences with others' homophobia and its impact on members' self-esteem and coping skills.

32. Help members identify and confront their own internalized homophobia while affirming the importance and validity of their sexuality.

33. Evaluate members for chemical dependence, and facilitate group discussion about the negative impact of illicit drugs on the immune system and on one's control over high-risk sexual behavior.

34. Refer chemically dependent group members to substance-abuse treatment programs.

35. If members refuse to commit to drug abstinence, teach them strategies for preventing the transmission of the HIV virus during drug use (e.g., not sharing needles, flushing the kit with bleach and then rinsing well), and encourage adherence to these strategies.

36. Elicit the expression of members' feelings about the loss of independence associ-

ated with prolonged HIV infection.

37. Facilitate group development of self-empowerment strategies, including increased self-care (self-nurturing activities), self-knowledge (learning all one can about one's medical situation and current available treatments), and self-advocacy (being willing and able to assertively push for the desired treatments).

38. Using role plays and behavioral rehearsal techniques, have members practice assertive advocacy behaviors in common, relevant scenarios.

39. Facilitate group exchange of information regarding social and community support networks. Add further information if necessary.

40. Facilitate group exchange of information regarding new experimental treatment protocols or current treatment strategies.

41. Facilitate group discussion of issues related to securing necessary medical care and attention.

42. Encourage the sharing of strategies for obtaining concrete medical and social services.

43. Encourage group members to ask each other for help with specific, concrete tasks and for emotional support.

44. Assign members to ask for help (concrete or emotional) during the week and report back to the group on their experiences.

45. Help group members clarify steps for continued self-care as they enlist the services of caregivers in the face of symptom progression.

46. Facilitate the development of contingency plans for own children in case of members' inability to care for them in the future.

47. Encourage members' expression of feelings (e.g., confusion and uncertainty) associated with long-term-survivor status (symptom-free or controlled symptom HIV infection for many years).

48. Facilitate group discussion about the impact of AIDS or HIV-positive status on career decisions, including the uncertainty resulting from long-term-survivor status.

49. Help group members develop realistic, short-term goals focusing on information gathering, lifestyle changes (e.g., exercise, nutrition, adequate rest), and developing a trusting relationship with a health care provider.

50. Elicit commitment to an ongoing program of good nutrition and general self-care.

—. _____
   _____
—. _____
   _____
—. _____
   _____

DIAGNOSTIC SUGGESTIONS

Axis I: 304.40   Amphetamine Dependence
              305.70   Amphetamine Abuse
              304.20   Cocaine Dependence
              305.60   Cocaine Abuse
              304.00   Opioid Dependence
              305.50   Opioid Abuse
              304.80   Polysubstance Dependence
              296.2x   Major Depressive Disorder, Single Episode
              309.0   Adjustment Disorder With Depressed Mood
              309.24   Adjustment Disorder With Anxiety
              309.28   Adjustment Disorder With Mixed Anxiety and
                          Depressed Mood
              V62.82   Bereavement
              316   Maladaptive Health Behaviors Affecting HIV
                          Infection
              316   Personality Factors Affecting HIV Infection
              316   Psychological Factors Affecting HIV Infection
              _____   _____
              _____   _____

INCEST OFFENDERS—ADULT

BEHAVIORAL DEFINITIONS

1. Sexual contact with a child with whom client has a trusting or parental relationship.
2. Inappropriate sexual "noncontact" (exhibitionism, voyeurism, obscene phone calls) with a child with whom client has a trusting or parental relationship.
3. Inappropriate intimacy expectations of the victim resulting from blurring of boundaries.
4. Recognition that the offending behavior is inappropriate.
5. Admission of responsibility for at least some aspect of the alleged sexual abuse.
6. Blaming of the victim or the circumstances for the sexual contact.
7. Major cognitive distortions about the victim resulting in rationalizing the sexual abuse.
8. Underdeveloped empathic skills.
9. Few significant relationships, including marital relationships.
10. Inability to establish and maintain meaningful social relationships.
11. No chronic sexual fixation on children (i.e., not a pedophile).

—. _____

_____

—. _____

_____

—. _____

_____

LONG-TERM GOALS

1. Acknowledge personal responsibility for own inappropriate sexual behavior and terminate sexual abuse.
2. Bear the consequences of the offending behavior (e.g., leave home, support the family, pay for the victim's therapy).
3. Break through the denial associated with the offending behavior and develop honesty with self and others.
4. Develop empathy with respect to the effects of the sexual abuse on the victim.
5. Understand the factors that led to the offending behavior and develop skills to prevent it from recurring (i.e., stop having sex with children).
6. Enter and remain in individual, marital (where still available), and family therapy.
7. Improve self-esteem and decrease feelings of worthlessness.
8. Develop appropriate significant relationships with spouse, friends, and others.
9. Develop coping strategies that minimize the risk of relapse.

—. _____

   _____

—. _____

   _____

—. _____

   _____

SHORT-TERM OBJECTIVES	THERAPEUTIC INTERVENTIONS
1. Each member verbalize the reason for participation in the group and the possible legal and other consequences that lie ahead. (1, 2)	1. Ask each group member to describe in detail his offenses and his current position vis-à-vis the criminal justice system.
2. Verbalize the factors that made the sexual behavior abusive and inappropriate versus consensual and appropriate. (3)	2. Facilitate group confrontation of any speaker's denial, rationalization, and minimization of his sexually abusive behavior.

3. Verbally compare the facts of the sexual abuse with the commonly accepted myths of sexual abuse. (4)

4. Verbalize an understanding of how sexual abuse occurs as a result of unresolved childhood issues and conflicts—not necessarily connected to sexual issues. (5)

5. Identify early painful experiences of abuse: physical, sexual or emotional, including experiences related to parental alcoholism or drug abuse. (6, 7)

6. Identify the negative thoughts and feelings that currently accompany childhood memories of abuse. (8)

7. Implement coping strategies to reduce the impact of negative thoughts and feelings on current behavior. (9, 10)

8. Keep a journal of daily stressful events and thoughts, feelings, and fantasies related to sexual abuse. (11)

9. Identify the events—usually involving a significant other person or a serious life stress—that trigger high-risk feelings of tension and anxiety and reflect childhood thoughts and feelings. (11)

10. Identify and confront the distorted thoughts occurring before, during, and after the abuse that justify the behavior. (12, 13)

3. Explain the factors that make sexual behavior between two people abusive (age differences, power differences, threat of physical harm, misuse of trust); ask group members to identify and discuss the factors involved in their own sexual offenses.

4. Discuss with group members the myths of sexual abuse (e.g., abusers must be "crazy"; they don't know their victims) and have members compare these myths with the realities of their own offenses.

5. Describe to the group the chain of events showing links between childhood abuse experiences, the painful emotions and cognitions that result, the current (adult) triggers of those painful emotions and cognitions, and the current coping strategies that lead to offending behavior.

6. Assign group members to list and share with the group childhood abuses (physical, sexual, or emotional) that can still arouse emotional pain.

7. Demonstrate and facilitate the expression of empathy with the speaker about the pain associated with his early abuses.

8. Help group members identify negative thoughts and feelings associated with the

11. Verbalize realistic cognitions about sexual abuse and the victim that avoid high-risk distortions. (14)

12. Verbalize an understanding of how the view of the victim as a supportive peer or surrogate partner is a distortion. (12, 13, 15)

13. Verbalize how sex can be an expression of power or control versus love and affection. (16)

14. Identify ongoing sexual thoughts regarding the victim. (17)

15. Report on the implementation of thought-stopping techniques to control inappropriate fantasies. (17, 18)

16. Replace negative thoughts about self with positive, self-affirming thought patterns. (19)

17. Acknowledge a pattern of alcohol or drug abuse and begin appropriate treatment. (20)

18. Verbalize the intent to terminate all sexual abuse and to not indulge associated fantasies. (21)

19. Acknowledge that knowing sexual abuse is wrong is not enough to prevent its recurrence. (12, 22)

20. Identify the chain of events involved in the relapse process that leads to reoffenses. (23)

early abuses. Encourage members to compare and contrast their own thoughts and feelings with those of the speaker.

9. Ask group members to explore with each other whether and how the thoughts and feelings that occur before each current sexual offense are the same as those associated with their childhood experiences of abuse.

10. Assist group members in identifying strategies to use in coping with negative thoughts and feelings that result in sexual offending behaviors (e.g., call another member of the group and talk about the thoughts and feelings, use thought-stopping techniques to stop the negative thoughts and resulting feelings, remove self from a situation that gives access to potential victims).

11. Assign group members to keep track every day of thoughts, feelings, and fantasies related to sexual abuse, including the stressful events that were happening around them before sexual thoughts or fantasies occurred. Have members read some of these daily logs to the group each week.

12. Have group members identify and discuss the cogni-

21. Identify and remove external stimuli that trigger relapse. (24)

22. Report on successful implementation of escape strategies when relapse risk is high. (25)

23. Practice the use of preventive cognitive self-talk during times of high risk for relapse. (26)

24. Increase understanding of the myths about the victim. (27)

25. Verbalize an increased understanding of the common emotional, behavioral, psychological, and physical reactions of victims of abuse. (28, 29)

26. Accurately express the immediate and long-term feelings of victims of sexual abuse. (30, 31)

27. Verbalize accurate information regarding appropriate, normal sexual development of children, adolescents, and adults. (12, 32)

28. Verbalize the difference between consent, coercion, and grooming. (33)

29. Discuss the abuse with family members without further traumatizing the victim and then make appropriate apologies to both the victim and other family members. (34, 35)

30. Increase the frequency of superficial communication

tive distortions they used to justify their sexual offenses.

13. Facilitate group confrontation of the speaker's inconsistencies in thinking.

14. Have group members develop reality-based cognitions to counter and replace the high-risk distortions.

15. Confront distorted view of the victim as a surrogate partner or peer.

16. Ask each group members to share his views of sex as an expression of love and closeness as opposed to power or dominance.

17. Monitor each group member's continuing sexual fantasies about the victim, pointing out the danger of indulging in such fantasies and encouraging the use of thought-stopping techniques (e.g., visualizing a stop sign, shouting "Stop" to self, replacing thoughts with alternative pleasant and appropriate ones).

18. Review and reinforce successful use of thought-stopping techniques to control inappropriate fantasies.

19. Explore with the group the negative cognitive messages about self that trigger feelings of worthlessness and facilitate the development of alternative positive cognitions.

with spouse/partner (if marriage is still viable). (36, 37)

31. Increase the frequency of intimate communication with spouse/partner. (38, 39)

32. Identify instances of being hurt or rejected by trusted women and relate these experiences to selecting a child as a sexual target. (40)

33. Express vulnerable feelings, private thoughts, and sexual fantasies. (11, 41, 42)

34. Decrease the time spent in isolation and increase frequency of social contacts. (41, 43, 44)

35. Implement assertiveness skills in the pursuit of meeting previously unmet needs. (45)

36. Verbalize the basic steps involved in problem solving and report on their application to specific conflicts in personal life. (46)

37. Practice the use of time-out techniques to modulate anger. (47)

—. _____
   _____
—. _____
   _____
—. _____
   _____

20. Evaluate each member's alcohol and drug use, and make appropriate referrals for treatment if indicated.

21. Ask each group member to make explicit his intent to terminate all sexual abuse and to not indulge in associated fantasies.

22. Emphasize the need for a multifaceted program (e.g., support-group participation, cognitive changes brought about through therapy, strict boundaries on relationships, avoidance of trigger situations) that supports termination of sexual abuse, not just a verbal pledge.

23. Describe the chain of events involved in the relapse process that leads to reoffenses. (For example, past hurts or abuses lead to negative feelings and thoughts about oneself, which result in the high-risk situations of rejection or humiliation that trigger the same negative thoughts and feelings, which induce coping mechanisms such as alcohol use to deal with the negative thoughts and feelings that facilitate the abuse, which in turn allow cognitive distortions about the victim and about the offending behavior that cause the abuse.) Encourage group members to identify and discuss the details of

their own personal relapse chain of events.

24. Ask group members to identify and commit to remove the external stimuli in their lives that facilitate relapse (avoiding child pornography, choosing a route to work that bypasses a local elementary school, etc.); have members report to the group on their compliance.

25. Engage group members in the development and rehearsal of escape strategies to use early in the relapse chain of events (e.g., using thought-stopping techniques; replacing negative cognitions with positive, self-affirming cognitions; physically removing self from high-risk situations).

26. Facilitate discussion of the perceived need for immediate gratification of sexual urges and the development of cognitive self-talk to combat these urges (e.g., "Two minutes of power are not worth twenty years in prison"; "I'll feel more ashamed of myself if I abuse this child"; "The victim will never forget the pain of the abuse").

27. Have group members discuss myths about victims (e.g., "If she doesn't resist, it isn't abuse"; "She really does like it as much as I do"; "She knows it's a way to show that I love her"; "She's

too young to remember any-thing").

28. Assign group members to read and discuss excerpts written by victims of sexual abuse.

29. Discuss with members the common reactions of victims to sexual abuse.

30. Facilitate the development of empathy for group members' victims by using role-reversal techniques to get perpetrators to express the feelings of their victims.

31. Assign each group member to write about the incest experience from the child's perspective. Have members read their papers aloud to the group.

32. Elicit group members' ideas and opinions about normal sexual behavior for children, adolescents, and adults, including the role of sexual fantasies; correct false information.

33. Clarify the differences between obtaining consent, using coercion, and grooming (or manipulating) a victim; help group members identify and discuss their own use of coercion and grooming in their offending behavior.

34. Ask each group member to write appropriate apologies to his victim and other family members. Have members read their apologies aloud to the group.

35. Assign each member to meet with his family to explain the chain of events, to verbally accept responsibility for his abusive behavior, and to make a verbal commitment to act differently in the future. After discussion with the family, assign the group member to read aloud his apologies.

36. Assign group members to spend five minutes daily talking with their spouse or partner about general day-to-day topics.

37. Ask group members to report to the group on their experience of talking with their spouse or partner on a superficial level.

38. Assign group members to spend five minutes a day talking about their thoughts, feelings, hopes, and fears with their spouse or partner.

39. Have group members report back to the group on their experience of talking with their spouse or partner on an emotional level.

40. Draw out members' early experiences of being hurt or rejected by trusted women; probe how these feelings could be related to the selection of a minor as a sexual target.

41. Facilitate appropriate, honest communication between group members.

42. Facilitate expressions of feelings among group members.

43. Assign small groups of members to practice social-skills exercises and role-play conversations; reinforce social-skills improvement.

44. Have group members practice maintaining eye contact while speaking; reinforce success.

45. Ask group members to clarify the distinction between assertion and aggression. Teach basic assertiveness skills and have members practice in small groups.

46. Teach problem-solving skills (i.e., identify the problem, brainstorm all possible options, evaluate each option and eliminate mutually intolerable options, select best remaining option, implement course of action, and evaluate results) and role-play their application to everyday life conflicts.

47. Teach the six components of the time-out technique (i.e., *self-monitoring* for escalating feelings of anger and hurt, *signaling* to the partner that verbal engagement should end, *acknowledging* the need of the partner to disengage, *separating* to disengage, *cooling down* to regain control of anger, and *returning* to controlled verbal engagement).

___. _____

_____

___. _____

_____

___. _____

_____

DIAGNOSTIC SUGGESTIONS

Axis I: V61.21   Sexual Abuse of Child
303.90   Alcohol Dependence
304.80   Polysubstance Dependence
302.2   Pedophilia, Limited to Incest

_____   _____

_____   _____

Axis II: 301.81   Narcissistic Personality Disorder
301.83   Borderline Personality Disorder

_____   _____

_____   _____

INCEST SURVIVORS—ADULT

BEHAVIORAL DEFINITIONS

1. Self-report of inappropriate sexual contact with an older family member (e.g., sibling, parent, or stepparent) during own childhood or adolescence.
2. Extreme difficulty becoming intimate with others.
3. Inability to enjoy sexual contact with desired partner.
4. Pervasive pattern of promiscuity or the sexualization of relationships.
5. Dissociative response to stressful situations.
6. Disproportionate response of anger, rage, or anxiety to stress.
7. Not actively suicidal or psychotic.
8. No history of substance abuse or in sustained full recovery from chemical dependence.
9. Concurrent participation in individual psychotherapy.

—. _____
_____
—. _____
_____
—. _____
_____

LONG-TERM GOALS

1. Talk about the sexual abuse and its consequences in one's life without being emotionally overwhelmed.
2. Overcome any feelings of guilt and shame while placing complete responsibility for the incest on the perpetrator.

3. Increase intimacy with others.
4. Increase enjoyment of sexual contact with desired partner.
5. Decrease pattern of promiscuity or inappropriate sexualization of relationships.
6. Better control the expression of feelings under stress.
7. Formulate goals for continuing the work of recovery in individual therapy.

—. _____
   _____
—. _____
   _____
—. _____
   _____

SHORT-TERM OBJECTIVES

1. State how own incest victimization has affected various arenas of life. (1)

2. Articulate individual goals for group treatment of sexual abuse. (2)

3. Practice self-calming exercises. (3, 4, 5)

4. Tell the entire story of the incest. (6, 8)

5. Describe self as an empowered survivor rather than a hopeless victim of sexual abuse. (7, 19, 41, 42)

6. Identify and express the feelings connected to the incest. (8)

7. Identify complex feelings about the perpetrator and other family members. (9, 11, 12)

THERAPEUTIC INTERVENTIONS

1. Ask each group member to describe ways in which the incest has affected her, her relationships, and her work.

2. Have group members state what they would like to accomplish in the group.

3. Encourage members to monitor their levels of stress to avoid feeling flooded and emotionally shutting down.

4. Lead group members through a safe-place visualization and encourage its practice whenever stressed.

5. Ask group members to develop a nonverbal signal to indicate when their feelings are too intense and they need a time-out.

8. Sort out and identify the complex feelings of guilt, shame, or anger toward self. (10, 11, 12)

9. Verbalize influence of incest experiences on present interactions. (13, 14)

10. Monitor feelings and reactions while in the process of recovery from incest. (15)

11. Differentiate between shame and guilt. (16)

12. Read and complete written exercise regarding guilt in *The Courage to Heal Workbook* (Davis). (17, 18)

13. Read books on incest and discuss important concepts. (19, 20)

14. Decrease statements of and reported feelings of self-blame for the incest, putting responsibility solely on the perpetrator. (21, 22, 23, 27)

15. Verbalize decrease in shameful feelings. (20, 24)

16. Give examples of the lack of proper boundaries in the family of origin. (25, 26)

17. Identify the various normal female childhood interactions with adult males. (27)

18. Identify three ways that incest is a betrayal. (28, 29)

19. Assertively express anger in controlled, appropriate fashion. (30, 31, 32)

20. Write a letter to perpetrator expressing various feelings that have resulted from sexual abuse. (33, 34)

6. Encourage group members to talk about their sexual abuse experiences in whatever detail they can tolerate.

7. Help members rewrite the endings of their stories in which they survive and master the experiences rather than being a hopeless victim.

8. Elicit feelings associated with the telling of the stories and with the abuse itself.

9. Explore with group members feelings about the perpetrator, about the parent who did not protect them, about the events that occurred when they told someone what had happened.

10. Explore feelings about submitting, participating, or even enjoying the sexual interactions. Help members express the positive as well as the negative feelings toward self and others.

11. Model and facilitate giving supportive feedback.

12. Facilitate sharing of similar experiences by group members.

13. Explore with group members current situations that remind them of the past.

14. Compare group members being the center of attention in the group with being the center of attention in their families.

21. Write a letter to nonprotective parent expressing feelings generated by the sexual abuse. (35, 36)

22. Report a decrease in the use of dissociation as response to stress. (37, 38)

23. Increase the frequency of self-nurturing behavior. (39, 40)

24. Verbalize an increased awareness of choices. (41, 42)

25. Demonstrate assertiveness skills, including those needed in negotiating for personal needs and desires. (43, 44)

26. State examples of an increase in the trust of self and others. (45, 46)

27. Verbalize an increased understanding of the issues involved in confronting the abuser. (47, 48)

28. Report an increased tolerance and enjoyment of sexual intimacy. (49)

29. Verbalize strategies for avoiding repetition of the abuse in relationships. (50)

___. _____
    _____

___. _____
    _____

___. _____
    _____

15. Assign group members to keep a journal recording memories or flashbacks stirred by the group, and feelings elicited about those memories.

16. Facilitate group discussion about the distinction between guilt ("I did something really bad") and shame ("I'm a really bad person").

17. Assign group members to complete written exercise regarding overcoming guilt in *The Courage to Heal Workbook* (Davis).

18. Encourage group discussion about the written exercise.

19. Assign members to read chapters from *The Courage to Heal* (Bass and Davis) and *Outgrowing the Pain* (Gil) and discuss responses with the group.

20. Assign group members to read sections in *Healing the Shame That Binds You* (Bradshaw) and discuss reactions in the group.

21. Clarify with group members that responsibility for the incest lies solely with the perpetrator.

22. Question members' statements of self-blame and the beliefs underlying the statements.

23. Teach group members that blaming themselves allows an illusion of control.

24. Teach group members the concept of shame as a means of behavioral control.

25. Provide information to group members about incest families and the lack of boundaries.

26. Elicit examples from members about the boundary problems in their own families of origin.

27. Facilitate group discussion about normal childhood behavior (e.g., girls flirting with fathers) and responsibility for the abuse.

28. Teach group members about incest as a threefold betrayal of the child: betrayal by the perpetrator for his own sexual pleasure; betrayal by the mother for not protecting against the abuse; betrayal of one's own body for becoming aroused and enjoying the sexual stimulation.

29. Encourage group exploration of the betrayals of incest, stressing the responsibility of parents to protect their children from all such betrayals (including too-early sexual pleasure).

30. Help group members identify their anger in response to current as well as past situations.

31. Explore with group members how anger was treated in their families.

32. Normalize the experience of anger and model appropri-

ate expression of anger in the group.

33. Assign group members to write a letter (not to be sent) to their abuser expressing everything they ever wanted to say to him.

34. Elicit members' responses to writing a letter to the perpetrator.

35. Assign group members to write a letter (not to be sent) to the parent who did not protect them.

36. Elicit members' responses to writing a letter to the nonprotective parent.

37. Teach group members about dissociation as a coping strategy for incest survivors when under stress.

38. Help group members develop an awareness of their own tendency to dissociate, and encourage use of other strategies such as asking for time-out.

39. Explore with group members their unmet needs and desires, emphasizing the need for being responsible for taking care of themselves as adults.

40. Help members develop a list of self-nurturing behaviors and assign them to do two things from their list every day.

41. Confront members' statements expressing a lack of choice in their lives.

42. Help group members recognize the existence of alternatives, however undesirable, as a means of empowering themselves.

43. Use role playing, modeling, and behavioral rehearsal to teach group members assertive skills, including the skill of negotiating, distinguishing between compromise and sacrifice.

44. Have group members role-play, in dyads, negotiating for personal needs and desires.

45. Facilitate group discussion about the difficulty of trusting one's own judgment or trusting others, teaching the share-check method of assessing others' trustworthiness.

46. Elicit from members examples in their current lives of progress in the area of trusting self and others.

47. Discuss with group members the issue of confronting the abuser. Teach that such confrontations are often unsatisfying in that families usually respond in the same ways as they have to all other issues (by denial, minimizing, scapegoating, etc.).

48. Help group members identify the dynamics of their own family and the chances of a satisfying confrontation.

49. Facilitate group discussion about the impact of sexual

abuse in childhood on sexual intimacy in adulthood. Explore the value of talking with their sexual partners about the incest and negotiating for what they want sexually.

50. Discuss with group members their strategies for avoiding repetition of the abuse (e.g., setting appropriate boundaries or limits, recognizing choices, negotiating for compromise).

—. _____

_____

—. _____

_____

—. _____

_____

DIAGNOSTIC SUGGESTIONS

Axis I: 995.5   Sexual Abuse of Child
300.4   Dysthymic Disorder
300.15   Dissociative Disorder NOS
300.02   Generalized Anxiety Disorder

_____   _____

_____   _____

Axis II: 301.6   Dependent Personality Disorder
301.82   Avoidant Personality Disorder
301.83   Borderline Personality Disorder
301.81   Narcissistic Personality Disorder

_____   _____

_____   _____

INFERTILITY

BEHAVIORAL DEFINITIONS

1. Inability to conceive after one full year of heterosexual intercourse at a frequency of one to two times per week without the use of any contraception.
2. Damage to the reproductive organs (e.g., fallopian tubes, lining of the uterus, eggs, testicles, or sperm ducts) from injury, infection, drug use, surgery, or fibroid tumors.
3. Reduced fertility resulting from delayed childbearing.
4. Infertility arising from various physician-diagnosed physiological problems (e.g., hormonal problems, abnormal ovulation, inadequate hormonal stimulation, varicocele on testicle, antibodies or allergies to partner's sperm, inability to produce cervical mucus needed for passage of sperm).
5. Feelings of shame, frustration, grief, and depression resulting from infertility experience.
6. Loss of sexual pleasure as the result of repeated failed attempts to achieve pregnancy.
7. Feelings of guilt on the part of the infertile partner; anger on the part of the fertile partner.
8. Feelings of anxiety and confusion in the face of available treatment options.

—. _____
_____

—. _____
_____

—. _____
_____

LONG-TERM GOALS

1. Begin and maintain a healthy grieving process for the loss of the dream of carrying own biological child.
2. Clarify goals with respect to treatment options and take steps toward meeting those goals.
3. Replace feelings of shame, frustration, guilt, and anger with acceptance of the infertility problems.
4. Reduce the stress associated with the emotional, physical, and financial roller coaster of pursuing assisted reproductive techniques.

___. _____

_____

___. _____

_____

___. _____

_____

SHORT-TERM OBJECTIVES

1. Verbalize stressors associated with infertility that led to joining group. (1)
2. Describe the history of infertility struggles. (2)
3. Demonstrate the ability to give and receive empathic emotional support. (3)
4. Identify the feelings generated by infertility problems. (4, 5, 6)
5. Describe impact of infertility struggles on work and personal life. (7, 8, 9)
6. Identify the impact of infertility on relationship with spouse/partner. (9)
7. Verbalize the personal meaning of becoming a par-

THERAPEUTIC INTERVENTIONS

1. Ask each group member to describe their struggles with infertility that precipitated joining the group.
2. Elicit from group members their stories of attempts to conceive, including when help was sought, how a diagnosis was made, and available treatment options.
3. Offer, and facilitate other members offering, empathic emotional support to speaker.
4. Reinforce appropriate expression of feelings resulting from the problems of infertility (e.g., shame, frustration, grief, depression,

ent and the meaning of conceiving own biological child. (10, 11)

8. Verbalize an understanding of the concept of grief as a process that must be experienced in order to heal. (12)

9. Identify own position in the grief process. (13)

10. Demonstrate stress-reduction techniques of abdominal breathing and progressive muscle relaxation. (14, 15)

11. Replace cognitive distortions leading to feelings of hopelessness and shame with realistic, self-affirming cognitions. (16, 17, 20)

12. Using Socratic questioning, challenge beliefs that fuel cognitive distortions regarding infertility. (18, 19, 20)

13. Verbalize the impact of constant interfacing with the medical profession over the private business of conceiving a child. (21)

14. Demonstrate assertive communication skills in group and then with significant others. (22, 23, 24)

15. Ask for emotional support in group and then from significant others. (25)

16. Clarify treatment options for own infertility problems. (26)

17. Identify own fears associated with different treatment options. (27, 28)

isolation, hopelessness, anger).

5. Facilitate group discussion about the emotional impact of infertility, using examples from speakers' personal experiences.

6. Elicit from group members a description of the ways members have attempted to cope with the feelings generated by infertility problems.

7. Encourage group members to share their personal histories of ways in which infertility problems have impacted their work and personal life. Help members clarify the impact on their relationships with friends and family.

8. Facilitate group discussion about the pain and isolation experienced in the company of friends, family, and their children.

9. Elicit from group members the different reactions to the infertility problem of self and spouse/partner, including the conflicts generated by these differences; assess the need for referral for conjoint couples therapy.

10. Facilitate group discussion about the meaning (emotional, spiritual, biological) of becoming a parent. Encourage members to compare their own beliefs with those of the speaker.

18. Identify feelings associated with adoption. (29)

19. List the ramifications (emotional, physical, and financial) of different options. (30, 31)

20. Clarify the privacy-versus-secrecy issues involved in adoption and gamete donation. (32, 33, 34)

21. Verbalize an awareness of the ethical and moral considerations involved in third-party reproduction situations. (34, 35)

22. Identify roles and meaning to life that exist apart from being a parent. (36)

23. List potential benefits of not being a parent. (37)

24. Identify spiritual resources that can bring increased peace and acceptance to the pain of infertility. (38)

—. _____
_____

—. _____
_____

—. _____
_____

11. Elicit from group members the meaning for them of conceiving own biological child.

12. Teach group members that grief is a process rather than a stable thing, and describe the stages that most people experience: *shock* (including disbelief and numbness), *disorganization* (including anger, helplessness, guilt, fear, anxiety, sadness, despair, confusion, and disorientation), and *reorganization* (including taking action, meeting challenges, coping with fears, releasing sadness, changing values, and acceptance). Stress to members that the stages of grief neither follow any rigid order nor are independent from each other.

13. Encourage group members to share their experiences of grieving the losses associated with infertility (relinquishing dreams of a natural conception of a biological child, of carrying a pregnancy, etc.). Assist members in identifying their position in the grief process.

14. Lead group members through abdominal breathing and progressive relaxation protocols.

15. Assign members to practice breathing and relaxation techniques daily and report

back to the group on their experiences.

16. Help group members identify the negative, distorted cognitions that contribute to feelings of shame, frustration, guilt, anger, and hopelessness.

17. Facilitate the development of realistic, self-affirming cognitions to replace the cognitive distortions.

18. Assist members in identifying the beliefs that fuel the cognitive distortions (e.g., "I'm not a real man if I can't make my wife pregnant"; "There's something wrong with me if I can't conceive easily"; "Life is meaningless if I can't have a biological child") regarding infertility.

19. Teach Socratic questioning and encourage group members to challenge the beliefs that fuel their negative distortions.

20. Assign group members to use cognitive restructuring techniques *in vivo,* and periodically review their success.

21. Encourage group members to share the impact of having to seek medical help for the usually very private process of conceiving a child; encourage the use of cognitive restructuring to aid in coping.

22. Teach assertive communication techniques, including active listening and as-

sertive feeling statements (e.g., "I feel like _____ when you _____, and I would like _____").

23. Using role play and behavioral rehearsal, have group members practice assertive communication skills in dyads.

24. Assign group members to use active listening and assertive feeling statements *in vivo* and report back to the group on their success.

25. Facilitate group members asking directly for emotional support within the group, and encourage them to do the same with significant others in their lives.

26. Facilitate group discussion of the different treatment options available for different infertility problems. Encourage members to identify those options pertaining to their particular problems.

27. Elicit group members' fears (fear of not being able to love a child who is not a genetic offspring, fear of the child not loving them, fear of the medical problems that might arise for a child with unknown biological parentage, etc.) associated with relevant treatment options (artificial insemination with unknown donor sperm or eggs, surrogate mother, etc.).

28. Facilitate group discussion about strategies for coping with fears of using assisted reproductive techniques.

29. Explore feelings associated with the adoption option.

30. Encourage group brainstorming of the emotional, physical, and financial ramifications of pursuing different infertility treatment options (e.g., invasive surgical procedures, emotional roller coasters resulting from hormone stimulation, tremendous disappointments if birth mother changes her mind about the adoption, huge financial investments with no guarantee of success).

31. Facilitate group discussion about the emotional impact of accepting a child-free life as a result of infertility problems. (loss of identity as a parent, more focus on the relationship with partner as the primary source of love and satisfaction, a need to adjust values, etc.).

32. Elicit group members' ideas and fears about privacy versus secrecy as it pertains to telling an adopted child or one conceived through gamete donation or surrogacy about his/her genetic origins.

33. Inform group members about the negative impact of family secrets on the

mental health of children in those families.

34. Facilitate group discussion about a person's rights to information about him/herself, including origins and genetic inheritance.

35. Facilitate group discussion about the moral and ethical considerations involved in third-party reproductive situations (the creation of children—at great expense when there are so many adoptable children needing homes, the creation of many half siblings to different parents, the commercialization of embryos in embryo adoption, etc.).

36. Ask members to identify sources of meaning and other roles that provide fulfillment if the parenting option is given up.

37. Encourage group members to list any potential benefits of not being a parent (e.g., increased focus on a career, time available for service to others, avoidance of the risks of pain and disappointment from children, more time and energy available for partner relationship, avoidance of partner conflict over parenting).

38. Facilitate group discussion of spiritual resources members might use to find peace

with infertility after resolving any anger at God for the
problem.

—. _____

_____

—. _____

_____

—. _____

_____

DIAGNOSTIC SUGGESTIONS

Axis I: 296.2x   Major Depressive Disorder, Single Episode
309.0   Adjustment Disorder With Depressed Mood
309.24   Adjustment Disorder With Anxiety
309.28   Adjustment Disorder With Mixed Anxiety and
Depressed Mood
V62.89   Phase of Life Problem

_____   _____

_____   _____

PARENTING PROBLEMS

BEHAVIORAL DEFINITIONS

1. Inability to elicit cooperative, appropriate behavior from children.
2. Constant or frequent conflict with children.
3. Rigid, authoritarian style of enforcing obedience.
4. A lack of consistent behavioral limits and follow-through with consequences for misbehavior.
5. Poor communication and problem-solving skills.
6. Feelings of helplessness and despair about parenting skills.
7. Conflict between parents over methods and goals of parenting.

—. _____
   _____

—. _____
   _____

—. _____
   _____

LONG-TERM GOALS

1. Ability to elicit appropriate, cooperative behavior from children.
2. Develop authoritative style of parenting: loving support coupled with consistent, firm limits.
3. Greater confidence about parenting skills.
4. Lower frequency of conflicts mediated by problem-solving and assertive communication skills.

—. _____
   _____

—. _____

_____

_____

—. _____

_____

SHORT-TERM OBJECTIVES

1. Each person state some of the problems he/she has had with parenting. (1)

2. Identify a positive trait of each child in the family. (2)

3. Clarify the distinction between authoritarian, permissive, and authoritative styles of parenting. (3, 4)

4. Verbalize an understanding of the family system concept of changing self to elicit change from another. (5, 6)

5. Verbalize the four mistaken beliefs of misbehaving children. (7, 8)

6. Verbalize an understanding of how to identify a child's underlying mistaken belief. (9)

7. Identify mistaken beliefs of own acting-out children. (10, 11, 12)

8. Verbalize an understanding of the use of positive reinforcement in eliciting desired behavior in children. (13, 14)

9. Verbalize an understanding of different reinforcement strategies in eliciting posi-

THERAPEUTIC INTERVENTIONS

1. Ask each person to introduce him/herself, describing the problems in parenting that motivated him/her to join a parenting group.

2. Ask each person to describe a behavior or incident that illustrates what he/she likes most about his/her problem child or children.

3. Teach group members the three major styles of parenting (authoritarian, permissive, and authoritative) and explore whose needs are addressed in each.

4. Using role plays, have members demonstrate the authoritarian, permissive, and authoritative parenting styles to the rest of the group. Explore with members the feelings associated with each different style.

5. Teach group members that the most effective way of eliciting changes in their children's behavior is to change their own behavior.

6. Facilitate group discussion about the concept of changing own behavior to elicit change from one's children.

tive behaviors in children.
(15, 16)

10. Report successful use of reinforcement strategies to increase positive behaviors
and decrease negative be-
haviors with own children.
(17, 18)

11. Verbalize acceptance of
the principle that intrinsic
worth of children is not dependent on their behavior.
(19, 20, 21)

12. Articulate an understanding of the role of encouragement in increasing
cooperation. (22, 23, 24)

13. Report successful use of encouragement with children
displaying inadequacy. (25)

14. Demonstrate active listening skills. (26, 27, 30)

15. Increase the use of problem-
solving skills. (28, 29, 30)

16. Verbalize the limits of punishment as a useful disciplinary tool. (31, 32)

17. Demonstrate use of choice
as means of avoiding power
struggles with children.
(33, 34)

18. Differentiate between natural and logical conse-
quences to a child's
misbehavior. (35, 36)

19. Demonstrate skill in developing appropriate logical
consequences for a child's
misbehavior. (37, 38, 39)

20. Report increased use of
choices and consequences
with children. (38, 39)

Stress that initially
changes will elicit worse behavior from children, but
that perseverance will lead
to success.

7. Teach the four mistaken
beliefs that children can
develop that lead to misbehavior: that they can be-
long and feel worthy only
by receiving complete
parental *attention;* that
they can belong and feel
worthy only by being *powerful* and by subjugating a
parent; that they're totally
unlovable and feel so hurt
from the rejection that they
want to get *revenge* by
hurting back; that they
must be perfect to be worthy, and because that is im-
possible, they must avoid
expectations by being to-
tally *inadequate.*

8. Facilitate group discussion
about children's need to belong and feel worthy as it
relates to the four mistaken
beliefs that can arise from
that need.

9. Teach group members the
two diagnostic observations
required to identify the
mistaken belief underlying
the misbehavior of a particular child. (1) *Parent's feelings* about child's behavior
lead to (2) a parental response that initiates the
following *reaction from
child:* Attention-seeking behavior leads to parent feeling irritated, and parent

21. Verbalize and report appropriate use of time-out as a disciplinary tool. (40, 41, 42)

22. Differentiate who owns a particular problem according to whose rights are being violated. (43, 44)

23. Identify parenting response in different situations according to who owns the problem. (45, 46, 47, 48)

24. Implement appropriate parenting responses as guided by problem ownership. (49, 50)

—. _____

    _____

—. _____

    _____

—. _____

    _____

response brings only temporary termination of behavior; *power* seeking leads to anger, and limit-setting response brings power struggles; *vengeful* behavior leads to hurt, and punishment brings more revenge; *inadequacy* behavior leads to helplessness in parent, and attempts to assist child lead to more resistance.

10. Elicit examples from group members of their children's misbehavior and help them identify the child's underlying mistaken belief using the two diagnostic observations.

11. Assign group members to practice *in vivo* diagnosing of their children's misbehavior by observing their own feelings in response to their children's misbehavior and seeing what happens when they intervene.

12. Have members report back to the rest of the group regarding their attempts to diagnose the cause of their children's misbehavior.

13. Teach group members the three requirements of reinforcement: It must be *age-appropriate, proportionate* to the task at hand, and occur *immediately* following the desired behavior.

14. Facilitate group discussion of appropriate reinforcements for children of differ-

ent ages exhibiting behaviors of varying severity. Stress the power of parental attention, both positive (a smile, a caress) and negative (a sharp look, a slap).

15. Teach group members three alternative ways to increase desired behavior and decrease undesired behavior in their children: shaping (reinforcing ever closer manifestations of the desired behavior), reinforcing an incompatible behavior, and reinforcing anything but unwanted behaviors.

16. Elicit from group members examples of their children's problem behaviors, and brainstorm possible approaches to their resolution using the four reinforcement strategies (positive reinforcement of desired behavior, shaping, reinforcing an incompatible behavior, and reinforcing anything but the unwanted behavior).

17. Assist group members in carefully defining a positive or negative behavior, and then assign them to attempt to either increase or decrease it using the reinforcement skills.

18. Review group members' use of reinforcement, celebrating success in use of the skills and redirecting unsuccessful attempts.

19. Emphasize to group members that children's intrinsic worth as people is not dependent on how they behave and that all children misbehave at times.

20. Using members' examples, explore ways they can support a child's inherent worth while simultaneously giving feedback on his/her behavior (e.g., "Ashley, I love you very much but I will not accept your whining").

21. During the week, have group members practice responding to their children in ways that separate their worth as people from their behavior.

22. Teach group members about encouragement and working alongside of a child (rather than just giving authoritarian directives) as a means of helping children feel better about themselves, their role in the family, and the value of their contributions.

23. Elicit examples from group members of discouraged behavior and brainstorm encouraging responses.

24. Have members role-play, in dyads, their automatic responses to their children's displays of inadequacy. Ask the person role-playing the child to give feedback about how it feels to hear the automatic response. Then have members practice

making truly encouraging responses.

25. Assign members to practice encouraging their children during the week, whether or not they seem discouraged, and report back to the group the following week.

26. Teach group members active listening skills, including *listening with complete attention and good eye contact, listening to and acknowledging the feelings* (including negative feelings) the child is expressing, and then *expressing own feelings in "I" statements* ("I feel _____ when you _____, and I would like _____").

27. Have group members role-play active listening skills.

28. Teach group members the five steps of problem solving: *Define* the problem in specific terms; *brainstorm* alternatives; *choose* a mutually acceptable alternative; *develop* a plan to put the chosen alternative into practice, including a fallback plan; *evaluate* success of chosen alternative.

29. Using role plays, have group members practice the five problem-solving steps.

30. Assign members to practice active listening and problem-solving skills during the week and report back to the group the following week.

31. Elicit examples from group members of personal attempts to induce responsible, cooperative behavior from their children by using punishment.

32. Teach group members the limitations of punishment as a disciplinary tool (e.g., promotes a desire for revenge, decreases child's self-esteem, does not teach or reinforce desired behavior, increases emotional distance between parent and child).

33. Facilitate group discussion about ways of giving children choices between two or more parent-selected, -approved, and -controlled alternatives that increase the child's sense of responsibility and control.

34. Using role plays, have group members practice avoiding power struggles by offering choices.

35. Clarify for group members the difference between natural consequences (those that will occur without parental intervention) and logical consequences (those that require parental intervention) of a child's misbehavior.

36. Teach the three requirements of logical consequences: that they must be *related* to the misbehavior, *consistent* (with respect to follow through), and presented *without anger*.

37. Elicit examples of misbehavior from group members, and using brainstorming and behavioral rehearsal, practice formulating and setting appropriate logical consequences.

38. Assign group members to practice *in vivo* offering choices to and setting logical consequences for their children (or letting natural consequences have their impact).

39. Review group members' experiences of giving choices and setting consequences; reward successful experiences and redirect unsuccessful attempts.

40. Teach the appropriate use of time-out with children as either one of two alternatives offered in a choice ("You can play quietly here or you may play alone in your room") or as a logical consequence of behaving inappropriately around others.

41. Facilitate group discussion about the use of time-out with own children.

42. Assign members to use time-out as a disciplinary tool during the week and report back to the group about their experiences.

43. To determine who owns a problem, teach group members to differentiate between whether the parent's or the child's rights are being violated. For example,

if child isn't completing household chores, isn't coming home at the agreed-upon time, or uses parent's belongings without asking, then the parent's rights are being violated. If child has a fight with a friend, doesn't want to finish dinner, or wants to wear his/her hair in a particular style, then the child owns the problem (i.e., parent's rights are not being violated).

44. Using examples of problematic situations elicited from group members, have them decide who owns each problem. Emphasize to members that treating their children with respect involves accepting their differences and allowing them to make their own choices, providing that their health or safety is not at risk and the rights of others are not violated.

45. Teach that when the child owns the problem, appropriate responses are to listen and validate child's feelings and encourage problem solving.

46. Teach that when the parent owns the problem, he/she should express feelings in "I" statements, engage child in problem solving, and determine consequences.

47. Teach that when ownership of the problem is unclear or when both own the problem, an appropriate response is

to start with the child's problem, and if resolving child's problem doesn't resolve parent's, continue by expressing feelings and setting consequences.

48. Elicit examples of problem situations from group members and determine appropriate strategies according to who owns the problem.

49. Assign group members to practice *in vivo* determining who owns the problem and responding accordingly.

50. Review members' experiences of determining who owns the problem; reward successful responses while redirecting unsuccessful responses.

__. _____

_____

__. _____

_____

__. _____

DIAGNOSTIC SUGGESTIONS

Axis I: V61.20   Parent-Child Relational Problem

V61.8   Sibling Relationship Problem

V71.02   Child or Adolescent Antisocial Behavior

V62.3   Academic Problem

_____   _____

_____   _____

Axis II: V71.09   No Diagnosis on Axis II

_____   _____

_____   _____

PHOBIAS—SPECIFIC/SOCIAL

BEHAVIORAL DEFINITIONS

1. A persistent and unreasonable fear of a specific object or situation that promotes avoidance behaviors because an encounter with the phobic stimulus provokes an immediate anxiety response.
2. Avoidance of the phobic stimulus or feared environment results in marked distress or interference with normal routines, work, or relationships.
3. Hypersensitivity to the criticism or disapproval of others.
4. Reluctant involvement in social situations out of fear of saying or doing something foolish or of becoming emotional in front of others.
5. Increased heart rate, sweating, dry mouth, muscle tension, and shakiness in most social situations.
6. Overall pattern of social anxiety, shyness, or timidity that presents itself in most social situations.
7. Persistence of fear in spite of recognitions that the fear is unreasonable.
8. Mild depression in the face of decreased range of activities.
9. Prevalence of anxiety-provoking self-talk around feared object or situation.

—. _____

_____

—. _____

_____

—. _____

_____

LONG-TERM GOALS

1. Reduce fear of the specific stimulus object or situation that previously provoked immediate anxiety.
2. Eliminate interference in normal routines and remove distress from feared object or situation.
3. Replace anxiety-provoking cognitions with reality-based, self-affirming cognitions.
4. Interact socially without excessive fear or anxiety.
5. Develop the essential social skills that will enhance the quality of relationship life.

—. _____

_____

—. _____

_____

—. _____

_____

SHORT-TERM OBJECTIVES

1. Verbalize phobic fears that form the basis for joining a phobia group. (1)
2. Verbalize an understanding and acceptance of the ground rules of the group. (2)
3. Describe the history of the phobia. (3)
4. Verbalize an understanding of the development of phobias and relate it to own experience. (4, 5)
5. Give support to and accept support from other members. (6)
6. Verbalize an understanding of the long-term, predispos-

THERAPEUTIC INTERVENTIONS

1. Have each member describe his/her phobic anxieties and the particular incident that precipitated joining a phobia group.
2. Explain and elicit verbal commitment to the ground rules, including the necessity of doing homework, the value of sharing progress from week to week without talking about specific anxiety symptoms, and the importance of avoiding unnecessary exposure to phobic objects or situations until appropriate skills have been learned.

ing factors that lead to phobias and relate them to own
experience. (7, 8)

7. Identify own level of cumulative stress and its relationship to a vulnerability
to phobic responses. (9, 10)

8. Describe first phobic response and its triggering
event or situation. (11)

9. Identify those elements
that maintain own phobia.
(12, 13)

10. Practice abdominal breathing and progressive relaxation to reduce stress level.
(14, 15, 17)

11. Implement visualization of
peaceful scene to reduce
stress. (16, 17)

12. Exercise aerobically at least
four times per week for at
least 20 to 30 minutes.
(18, 19, 20)

13. Verbalize an accurate understanding of the nature of
phobic reactions. (21, 22, 23)

14. Report success at accepting,
observing, and floating with
the feelings of panic when
they occur rather than
fighting them. (24, 25)

15. Use coping statements to
facilitate an attitude of
calm acceptance of panic reactions toward feared ob-
jects or situations. (26)

16. Use personal anxiety scale
to identify early stages of
phobic anxiety. (27, 28)

3. Facilitate group sharing of
members' histories of phobic responses, including
circumstantial triggers,
severity, symptom pattern,
chronicity, and attempts at
coping or resolution.

4. Teach group members the
two ways in which phobias
develop: (1) by *conditioning,*
in which a neutral object or
situation is repeatedly
paired with an anxiety-
provoking stimulus (perhaps
even a random panic at-
tack), which in turn causes
avoidance, which reduces
the anxiety, thus reinforcing
the avoidance behavior, or
(2) by a *specific traumatic
incident* that is followed by
avoidance behavior.

5. Encourage group members
to use the knowledge of how
phobias develop to explore
the development of their
own phobias.

6. Encourage group members
to give empathetic support
to each speaker.

7. Teach group members the
long-term predisposing
causes of anxiety (e.g., genetic predisposition, growing up in a family where
parents fostered overcau-
tiousness, perfectionism,
emotional insecurity and dependence or where parents
suppressed assertiveness).

8. Have group members share
the long-term predisposing
causes of anxiety that per-

17. Temporarily withdraw from a situation when anxiety level of 5 is reached and return to it when anxiety is reduced. (29, 30)

18. Report success using abdominal breathing to abort a phobic anxiety attack. (31)

19. Report success in using coping statements along with relaxation skills to reduce phobic anxiety. (32)

20. Verbalize an understanding of the concepts of sensitization and desensitization. (33)

21. Complete successful desensitization protocol using imagery. (34, 35, 36, 37)

22. Confront own resistance to undertaking exposure to a fear-inducing situation or tolerating anxiety in those situations. (38)

23. Complete successful *in vivo* desensitization, first with support person, then alone. (39, 40)

24. Reward self for small successes that demonstrate any progress at all. (41)

25. Identify negative, anxiety-provoking cognitions. (42)

26. Verbalize the types of cognitive distortions that trigger anxiety in the face of phobic stimulus. (43)

27. Develop reality-based, self-affirming cognitions to replace the cognitive distortions and anxiety-provoking self-talk. (44, 45, 46)

tain to their own experiences.

9. Facilitate group discussion about how stress accumulates when it is not dealt with and how it can lead to psychophysiological illnesses. Encourage members to identify their own cumulative levels of stress.

10. Assign group members to fill out a Holmes and Rahe stress chart to identify recent stressors that could be contributing to their anxiety.

11. Elicit from group members a description of their first phobic response and the event or situation that triggered it.

12. Teach group members the emotional, cognitive, and behavioral elements that maintain phobic anxiety (e.g., avoidance; self-talk that fosters anxiety; inability to assertively express feelings, needs, and wants; muscle tension).

13. Encourage members to share with the rest of the group those phobia-maintaining factors with which they identify.

14. Teach deep abdominal breathing technique, instructing members to inhale slowly and deeply, pause, and exhale slowly and completely.

15. Lead members through progressive relaxation protocol, where each muscle group is

28. Identify the mistaken beliefs that fuel anxiety-provoking cognitions. (47)

29. Report success in countering mistaken beliefs using Socratic questions and positive affirmations. (48, 49)

30. Identify and verbalize suppressed feelings. (50, 51, 52, 54)

31. Verbalize the difference between behaviors that are aggressive, passive, and assertive. (53)

32. Express feelings openly and honestly in group and then with significant others. (54)

33. Apply assertive problem-solving techniques to daily problems to reduce stress level. (53, 55)

34. Increase implementation of self-nurturing behaviors. (56, 57)

—. _____
   _____

—. _____
   _____

—. _____
   _____

first tightened and then relaxed; stress the need for daily practice.

16. Guide members through a visualization of a peaceful, relaxation-inducing scene, eliciting as many details of the scene as possible. Encourage members to practice visualization daily after relaxation protocol.

17. Review members' success in using progressive relaxation and visualization during the week.

18. Describe to group members the physiological and psychological impact of aerobic exercise (e.g., rapid metabolism of excess adrenaline and thyroxin in the bloodstream; enhanced oxygenation of blood and brain, leading to improved concentration; production of endorphins; reduced insomnia; increased feelings of well-being; reduced depression).

19. Help group members formulate exercise programs, building toward a goal of at least 20 to 30 minutes at least four days per week. (Recommend reading *Exercising Your Way to Better Mental Health* by Leith.)

20. Have members report back to the group on their progress in meeting their exercise commitment, rewarding successes and sup-

portively confronting resistance.

21. Teach the concept of the phobic anxiety attack cycle, in which the conditioned phobic object or situation (trigger) leads to physical symptoms of panic (e.g., heart palpitations, shortness of breath, sweating, dizziness, trembling, tightness in the chest). The negative thoughts that immediately follow the beginning of physical symptoms intensify the symptoms, which in turn leads to more negative, catastrophic thoughts, and finally results in full-blown phobic anxiety attack.

22. Elicit group members' experiences that conform to the phobic anxiety attack.

23. Present accurate information (e.g., that anxiety attacks are simply the fight-or-flight response occurring out of context; that they are not dangerous and will not result in heart attack, fainting, dizziness, or going crazy) to counter the myths regarding the nature of phobic panic reactions.

24. Introduce the concept of accepting and observing, rather than fighting, the panic reaction and floating with the "wave" of panic. Explain how the concomitants of the fight-or-flight response are time-limited

and will end of their own accord.

25. Assign group members to practice observing and floating with their feelings of panic when they occur. Have members report back to the group on their success.

26. Provide group members with a list of coping statements (e.g., "I can be anxious and still deal with this situation"; "This is just anxiety, it won't kill me"; "I've survived this before and I'll survive it now") to encourage acceptance and a willingness to float with the panic rather than fight.

27. Help group members develop a personal anxiety scale from 0 (calm and relaxed) to 10 (terror), using 5 (marked anxiety) as the point between tolerable anxiety and out-of-control panic. Have members identify personal specific physiological signs that indicate a potential panic reaction.

28. Ask group members to use personal anxiety scale to identify early stages of phobic panic reaction (5 or below), when intervention is still possible.

29. Explain to group members the concept that a phobia can be reinforced by staying near the object (or in the situation) while experiencing too-high levels of anxiety.

30. Teach group members the strategy of withdrawing temporarily from situations in which anxiety level 5 is reached and then returning after anxiety is reduced. Encourage members to use the withdrawal strategy when necessary and report back to the group on their experiences.

31. Assign group members to use abdominal breathing and relaxation during the week when anxiety levels are 5 or below to abort a phobic anxiety reaction. Have members report back to the group on their success.

32. Assign group members to choose three or four coping statements and practice them with abdominal breathing and relaxation, first in group and then *in vivo* during the week. Have members report back to the group on their success.

33. Teach group members the concepts of sensitization (i.e., staying in a situation while experiencing high anxiety) and desensitization (i.e., learning to remain relaxed in an anxiety-provoking situation) using both imagery and *in vivo* experiences.

34. Help group members construct an appropriate desensitization hierarchy for their phobic situation or

object from least to most
anxiety-provoking stimuli.
Encourage members to in-
clude reality-based details
of each step of the hierarchy.

35. Lead group members
through the steps of sys-
tematic desensitization, repeating the scene until it
no longer has the capacity
to raise anxiety levels
above level 1 of personal
anxiety scale before pro-
gressing to the next scene
in the hierarchy.

36. Assign group members to
continue working on the desensitization protocol every
day for 20 minutes.

37. Review members' success in
working on their desensitization hierarchies.

38. Facilitate group discussion
of possible resistance to the
discomfort and hard work of
in vivo desensitization, emphasizing the difference between avoidance and
temporary retreat, and
warning that sometimes
anxiety gets worse before it
gets better.

39. Assign group members to
begin *in vivo* desensitization, first accompanied by a
safe support person, then
alone.

40. Review group members'
success in the use of *in vivo*
desensitization.

41. Help members develop a
self-reward system for re-

inforcing small steps toward recovery.

42. Elicit from group members the negative, distorted cognitions that provoke and maintain anxiety.

43. Teach group members the major types of cognitive distortions: *overestimating* the odds of a bad outcome (e.g., "If I have to do it again, I'll die"); *catastrophizing* (e.g., "It would be intolerable if I had to leave the room"); *overgeneralizing* (e.g., "If it happened today, then it'll happen every other time"); *filtering* out the positive aspects to focus on the negative (e.g., "I knew I'd feel anxious if I came here— nothing's changed after all"); *should* statements that impose unrealistic expectations (e.g., "I should be able to do this without anxiety"). Encourage members to share the distortions that trigger their own anxiety. Recommend reading *Ten Days to Self-Esteem* (Burns).

44. Help members develop reality-based, self-affirming cognitions to challenge and replace distorted, anxiety-provoking cognitions.

45. Assign group members to practice *in vivo* challenging and replacing their distorted, negative, anxiety-provoking cognitions with realistic, self-affirming ones.

46. Review members' experiences with cognitive restructuring, reinforcing success and redirecting failures.

47. Explore with group members the underlying mistaken beliefs (e.g., "People won't like me if they see who I really am"; "I don't deserve to be happy"; "It's terrible to fail"; "I should (never) be _____") that fuel anxiety-provoking cognitions.

48. Challenge members' distorted, negative beliefs regarding self by using the Socratic method of questioning, and help them develop self-affirmations to counter the mistaken beliefs.

49. Assign group members to use their self-affirmations during the week to challenge mistaken beliefs, and have them report on their success.

50. Help each group member identify symptoms of his/her suppressed feelings (e.g., free-floating anxiety, depression, psychosomatic symptoms such as headaches, ulcers, or muscle tension).

51. Give group members a handout listing a large number of feelings; have them use the list as a reference in learning to label and talk about their feelings.

52. Teach group members steps to "tune in" to their bodies to identify their feelings (e.g., relaxing steps might include, paying attention to where in the body there are physical sensations, waiting and listening to whatever arises). Have them use the feelings list to clarify.

53. Clarify the distinction between passive, aggressive, and assertive behavior. Then role-play situations where members make assertive requests and set boundaries with their dyad partners.

54. Encourage honest, assertive expression of feelings in group and then with significant others.

55. Teach group members the five steps to assertive problem solving (i.e., identify problem, brainstorm all possible options, evaluate each option and eliminate mutually intolerable options, implement course of action from remaining options, and evaluate results); then role-play their application to everyday life conflicts.

56. Help members develop a list of self-nurturing behaviors (e.g., taking a bath, reading a book, getting a massage); assign daily completion of at least one item from the list.

57. Have members report to the
    group on their success in
    self-nurturing.

—. _____

    _____

—. _____

    _____

—. _____

    _____

DIAGNOSTIC SUGGESTIONS

Axis I: 300.29   Specific Phobia
                300.23   Social Phobia

                _____   _____

                _____   _____

Axis II: V71.09   No Diagnosis on Axis II

                _____   _____

                _____   _____

RAPE SURVIVORS

BEHAVIORAL DEFINITIONS

1. Self-report of incident where force or the threat of force was used to obtain sexual contact.
2. Feelings of self-blame for the assault.
3. Sense of violation of trust and safety.
4. Feelings of fear, shame, depression, distrust, and anger.
5. Sleep disturbance (e.g., insomnia, violent dreams).
6. Hypervigilance related to feelings of general distrust resulting from the assault.
7. Fear of rejection by significant others (e.g., spouse, boyfriend, parent).
8. Sexual dysfunction secondary to feelings of shame, anger, and distrust caused by assault.
9. Work or relationship disturbances.
10. Physical symptoms resulting from the assault (e.g., headaches, nausea, eating disorders, muscle tension).

—. _____
   _____
—. _____
   _____
—. _____
   _____

LONG-TERM GOALS

1. Reduce sense of isolation.
2. Reduce feelings of guilt, shame, anger, and powerlessness.
3. Increase feelings of self-esteem.

4. Increase understanding about phenomenon of rape and sexual violence.
5. Increase ability to trust.

—. _____

_____

—. _____

_____

—. _____

_____

SHORT-TERM OBJECTIVES

1. Each group member introduce herself and share one thing about herself. (1)

2. Verbalize acceptance of the ground rules of the group. (2)

3. Verbalize an increased understanding of sexual assault continuum. (3, 4)

4. List common and personal emotional/physical symptoms associated with sexual assault. (5, 6)

5. Tell personal story of sexual assault. (7, 8)

6. Terminate statements of personal responsibility for the rape. (9, 10, 14)

7. Practice "safe-place" visualization. (11, 12)

8. State a clear understanding of the cultural myths about rape and rape victims. (13)

9. Make statements that place clear responsibility for the

THERAPEUTIC INTERVENTIONS

1. Ask group members to introduce themselves, telling the rest of the group one thing (of their choosing) about themselves.

2. Describe ground rules for the group (e.g., confidentiality, no substance use, preferably no missed sessions) and ask each member to commit to upholding them.

3. Teach group members the continuum of sexual assault, from suggestive comments or gestures to unwanted touch to rape.

4. Help members understand that the *impact* of the offending behavior defines it as "sexual assault" regardless of where the behavior lies on the continuum (e.g., obscene comments, flashing, unwanted touch, or rape).

5. Teach group members the emotional and physical

sexual assault on the perpetrator. (9, 14)

10. Make statements that identify self as a "survivor," not
a "victim." (15, 16, 17)

11. State a clear understanding
of the cultural myths about
rapists. (18, 19)

12. Report increased acceptance
and tolerance of uncomfortable feelings associated with
the rape. (20, 21, 22)

13. Identify useful strategies
to deal with angry feelings
related to sexual assault.
(23, 31)

14. List ways to cope with feelings of sadness associated
with the rape. (24, 31)

15. Verbalize cognitive strategies to overcome guilt and
shame. (25, 31)

16. State behavioral and cognitive actions to deal with
feelings of fear. (26, 31)

17. Identify behavioral and cognitive steps to cope with
distrust. (27, 31)

18. List ways to overcome
feelings of worthlessness.
(28, 31)

19. Verbalize constructive
means to cope with and
gradually overcome the desire to withdraw. (29, 31)

20. Identify steps to take to
begin to overcome sexual
dysfunction related to the
rape. (30, 31)

21. Verbalize realistic goals regarding time it takes for recovery. (32)

symptoms associated with
sexual assault.

6. Encourage members to add
their own emotional and
physical reactions to the list.

7. Explain to group members
the need to share the story
of their rape in order to
begin healing; elicit each
member's story in as much
detail as possible.

8. Model verbal support and
nurturing as members
share personal assault
stories.

9. Gently confront members'
statements that assume
any kind of responsibility
for the rape.

10. Help group members identify negative thoughts and
feelings about themselves
resulting from the rape by
using pointed questions and
questioning the logic of
their responses.

11. Lead members through a
deep-breathing exercise culminating in a visualization
of a "safe place" (as each
member defines it) where
they can relax, trust, and
feel accepted.

12. Encourage group members
to practice the safe-place visualization during the week.

13. Encourage group discussion
of the cultural myths of
rape and rape victims (if
she was wearing attractive
or sexy clothes, she asked
for it; if she went into a

22. List ways to overcome rape's psychophysiological symptoms. (33)

23. Write a letter to perpetrator expressing feelings of pain, anger, and blame. (34)

24. Identify current position regarding forgiveness of perpetrator without feeling compelled by "shoulds" or "oughts." (35)

25. Accurately assess progress toward recovery. (36)

26. Actively seek support outside the group. (37)

—. _____
   _____

—. _____
   _____

—. _____
   _____

dark or isolated place, she invited it; if the offender was known, it couldn't really have been rape; if she didn't resist, she must have wanted it; if she drank too much, she should have known better, etc.). Emphasize that no matter what a woman says or does, she does not deserve to be sexually assaulted.

14. Stress to group members that the choice to assault belongs solely to the man. Reframe members' tendency to retain some responsibility as denial or avoidance of feelings of powerlessness.

15. Describe to group members the two elements of surviving rape: surviving the rape itself and surviving the aftermath of traumatic feelings; contrast the concept of *survival* with that of defeated *victim*.

16. Elicit from group members the defensive survival strategies used to cope with the rape (e.g., moving to a different neighborhood, installing more-secure locks, resisting sex, going emotionally numb, binge eating).

17. Encourage members to support others' survival strategies and to validate their own and others' coping styles.

18. Explore with group members common myths about

rapists (e.g., they are crazy; they look the part of bad men; they are from one particular racial group; they are unknown to the victim; they are unemployed or in low-income jobs).

19. Provide group members with reality-based information about rapists.

20. Teach group members that emotional volatility is part of healing from rape.

21. Facilitate group members' sharing of feelings experienced as result of the rape, and facilitate release of affect where possible.

22. Give (and encourage other group members to give) emotional support to the speaker through consistent eye contact, active listening, unconditional positive regard, and warm acceptance to help increase her ability to identify and express feelings.

23. Elicit from group members constructive strategies for dealing with anger (e.g., hitting a pillow, doing something physically demanding).

24. Elicit from group members useful strategies for dealing with sadness (e.g., crying without embarrassment, expressing grief to friends, writing letter to self, friend, or family members explaining source of sadness).

25. Elicit from group members useful strategies for dealing with guilt and shame (e.g., challenging distorted thoughts that trigger guilt, putting themselves in the role of another rape/assault survivor and asking self if she feels responsible for the assault).

26. Elicit from group members useful strategies for dealing with fear (e.g., sleeping with the light on, getting a dog, taking a friend along to places that elicit fear, engaging in empowering self-talk that generates confidence).

27. Elicit from group members useful strategies for dealing with mistrust (e.g., reserving trust for a while, spending time only with very trusted friends, building trust in small steps of "share and check").

28. Elicit from group members useful strategies for dealing with feelings of worthlessness (e.g., challenging distorted thoughts that trigger worthlessness, calling a loved one and asking for reassurance of caring, reminding self of those that appreciate you).

29. Elicit from group members useful strategies for dealing with social withdrawal (e.g., allowing self some time alone, doing a nurturing activity like a warm bubble

bath or getting hair styled, keeping in contact with only a small circle of trusted people at first).

30. Elicit from group members useful strategies for dealing with impaired sexuality (e.g., engaging only in sexual activity that feels safe, allowing partner to reassure you during lovemaking, asking partner for agreement that sexual activity be under your complete control regarding what, when, where, how often).

31. Encourage group members to keep a journal of their most disturbing feelings and share them with the group; urge feedback from group about ways to cope that have been successful for them.

32. Teach group members that recovery from rape—as from any major physical trauma (e.g., heart surgery)—takes time and energy.

33. Elicit examples of how members can address the psychophysiological symptoms resulting from the rape (e.g., by getting more rest, eating nurturing meals at regular times, slowing down, scaling back on activities).

34. Ask each member to write a letter to her rapist expressing feelings rape has engen-

dered; process letter within group.

35. Teach the healing power of forgiveness versus bitter hatred, but take extreme care not to excuse perpetrator or to pressure members beyond their need to hold perpetrator responsible and their own current feelings of anger; plant a seed that can grow with healing time.

36. Evaluate with group members their current symptomatology compared to that existing at the beginning of group therapy.

37. Encourage group members to seek continued support through individual therapy.

__. _____
   _____
__. _____
   _____
__. _____
   _____

DIAGNOSTIC SUGGESTIONS

Axis I:	995.81	Sexual Abuse of Adult
	309.81	Posttraumatic Stress Disorder
	309.xx	Adjustment Disorder
	296.2x	Major Depressive Disorder, Single Episode
	308.3	Acute Stress Disorder
	_____	_____
	_____	_____
Axis II:	V71.09	No Diagnosis on Axis II
	_____	_____
	_____	_____

SEPARATION AND DIVORCE

BEHAVIORAL DEFINITIONS

1. Decision to end the marriage (or the relationship, if not married).
2. Moving out of the home to establish separate living arrangements due to dissatisfaction with the relationship.
3. Initiation of legal proceedings for separation, divorce, and/or child custody.
4. Confusion about how best to deal with the feelings and welfare of the children.
5. Anger, hurt, and fear regarding breaking the partnership and having to face life as a single person.
6. Spiritual conflict over the breaking of marriage vows.
7. Depression and withdrawal as a part of the grief process related to the loss of the relationship.

—. _____

_____

—. _____

_____

—. _____

_____

LONG-TERM GOALS

1. Resolve the initial confusion and turmoil of separation.
2. Consistently uphold the best interests of the children as paramount in dealing with partner, and act accordingly.
3. Learn to cope with the varied losses that separation entails.
4. Mourn the end of the marriage adequately to facilitate cooperation with ex-partner in reaching a fair divorce agreement.

5. Reduce hurt and angry feelings.
6. Establish and maintain healthy coparenting practices with ex-partner.

—. _____

_____

—. _____

_____

—. _____

_____

SHORT-TERM OBJECTIVES

1. Introduce self and verbalize stresses related to separation/divorce that led to participating in divorce group. (1)
2. Describe the history of the relationship, culminating in its present state. (2, 3, 4)
3. Give empathic support to and accept support from other group members. (5, 7)
4. Verbalize the impact of divorce on children, personal and social life, and family relationships. (6, 7)
5. Identify cultural, religious, and spiritual meanings and ramifications of divorce. (8, 9)
6. Verbalize a commitment to being sensitive to children's thoughts, feelings, and needs during adjustment period. (10, 11, 12, 13)
7. Verbalize a plan for talking to the children about the divorce. (14, 15)

THERAPEUTIC INTERVENTIONS

1. Have each member introduce him/herself to the rest of the group and describe the stressful incident related to the divorce that precipitated joining the group.
2. Have members share with the group the developmental stages of their relationship (e.g., dating, early marriage, couple with young children, long-term marriage).
3. Elicit from group members the history of conflict in their relationships, including changes in marital happiness and precipitants to divorce.
4. Encourage group members' honest expression of feelings associated with the divorce.
5. Demonstrate and facilitate empathic support among group members.

8. Report on experience of talking to the children about the divorce. (16)

9. Identify the four major emotional stages of recovery from divorce and give personal examples of behaviors reflecting own stage of recovery. (17, 18)

10. Practice stress-reduction techniques to alleviate anxiety. (19, 22)

11. Identify distorted cognitions that contribute to depression, anxiety, and guilt. (20)

12. Replace distorted cognitions with realistic, self-affirming cognitions. (21)

13. Report decrease in depression, anxiety, and guilt using stress-reduction techniques and cognitive restructuring. (19, 21, 22)

14. Verbalize acceptance of the new social identity accompanying divorce. (23)

15. Implement strategies for coping with others' disapproval. (24, 25)

16. Identify own behavior that improved or harmed the relationship. (26, 27)

17. Express feelings, including anger, openly and honestly. (28)

18. Report a decrease in angry feelings brought about by using anger management tools. (29, 30, 31, 32)

19. Increase participation in social activities to reduce social isolation. (33)

6. Explore with group members the implications of divorce for their children, their personal lives, their social activities, and their extended families.

7. Encourage group members to relate their own experiences and situations to those of the speaker.

8. Help group members identify the cultural, religious, and spiritual meanings that divorce holds for them.

9. Facilitate group discussion of the ramifications of divorce from the cultural, religious, and spiritual perspectives.

10. Teach group members the impact of divorce on children, stressing the factors that maximize children's adjustment (e.g., keeping kids out of the middle of parental conflicts, including custody battles; remaining in a parental role and not turning to the child for emotional support; avoiding joining in child's anger toward other parent).

11. Encourage group discussion of ways to facilitate expression of and support children's thoughts, feelings, and needs (e.g., by spending quality time with child, being open about own feelings, asking child about his/her feelings and listening nonjudgmentally).

20. Write a letter to ex-partner (not to be mailed) expressing all the feelings associated with the divorce. (34, 35)

21. Develop a ritual to facilitate "letting go" of ex-partner. (36, 37)

22. Report an increase in the ability to ask for emotional support. (38, 39)

23. Describe ongoing reactions of children to the divorce and own ability to support children's feelings and needs. (40, 41)

24. Demonstrate active listening and assertive communication skills. (42)

___. _____
_____

___. _____
_____

___. _____
_____

12. Assign members to read books on coping—and helping children cope—with divorce (e.g., *The Divorce Book* by McKay, Rogers, Blades, and Gosse, *Mom's House, Dad's House* by Ricci) and discuss with group.

13. Encourage group members to verbally commit to upholding the best interests of the children as a guiding principle in maneuvering through divorce.

14. Facilitate group exploration of strategies for talking to children about divorce, stressing the importance of communicating to children that divorce is not their fault, that they are still loved, and that nothing they do can prevent the divorce or fix the problems in the relationship.

15. In small groups, have group members role-play communicating with their children about divorce issues.

16. Assign members to talk *in vivo* to their children about the divorce and report back to the group.

17. Teach group members the characteristics of the four major emotional stages of divorce: *separation shock* (characterized by numbness and denial, anxiety, and anger; *roller-coaster effects* (characterized by emotional volatility, changes in identity and self-perception,

loneliness, and assessment of the relationship); *identity work* (characterized by an adolescent-like narcissism and experimenting with new behaviors); *recentered self* (characterized by an integration of aspects of life to fit new perception of self).

18. Elicit from members examples of behaviors reflecting their personal stage of emotional recovery from divorce.

19. Teach group members deep abdominal breathing and progressive relaxation, and encourage them to practice daily.

20. Help group members identify the distorted, negative cognitions that trigger feelings of anxiety, depression, and guilt.

21. Assist group members in developing realistic, self-affirming cognitions to replace negative self-talk, and assign them to practice cognitive replacement *in vivo* during the week.

22. Review group members' success in reducing their anxiety, depression, and guilt using stress-reduction techniques and cognitive restructuring. Reinforce successful experiences and redirect unsuccessful attempts.

23. Facilitate group discussion of the changes in social identity brought about by divorce (e.g., greatly reduced

budget for social activities, loss of some friendships, no longer a homeowner, being a single parent).

24. Explore with group members the reactions of friends and extended family members to the divorce.

25. Teach group members strategies for coping with others' disapproval (e.g., keeping details of the divorce private, avoiding conflict by simply stating and restating position [broken-record technique], resisting asking others to take sides); encourage group discussion.

26. Elicit from group members personal examples of behaviors aimed at strengthening the relationship and those that contributed to the downfall of the relationship.

27. Confront speaker's denial, rationalization, or minimization of the impact of his/her hurtful behaviors.

28. Help group members identify their feelings and practice expressing them in assertive feeling statements ("I feel _____ when you _____ because I _____"; "I would like _____").

29. Teach group members that feelings of anger require both the experience of pain (physical or emotional) and trigger thoughts (attribu-

tions that blame others for the painful experience).

30. Help group members identify personal trigger thoughts about their ex-partner that elicit anger (e.g., "He's such a _____"; "If it weren't for her, I wouldn't be living like this").

31. Facilitate development of general coping statements (e.g., "I must go on with my life"; "There's no payoff in blaming my ex"; "My anger hurts me more than it hurts him/her so I might as well release it").

32. Review group members' experiences of using coping statements to reduce anger; reinforce successes and gently confront unsuccessful attempts.

33. Assign members to participate in at least one social activity during the week and report back to the rest of the group.

34. Assign group members to write a letter (not to be sent) to their ex-partner expressing everything they always wanted to say to him/her about the relationship and the divorce.

35. Elicit and process members' responses to writing a letter to their ex-partners, allowing them to read it to the group, if desired.

36. Facilitate group discussion about the value of a ritual to "bury" the past, (e.g., burying or burning old love letters, mementos, and photos—saying goodbye to each piece).

37. Encourage group members to carry out their own private ritual when ready and report back to the group about the experience.

38. Elicit group members' fears of asking for emotional support from friends and family members. Help them evaluate appropriate sources of such support (e.g., friends who were less involved with both members of the relationship, family members with whom a separate relationship was maintained).

39. Assign group members to ask one person during the week for emotional support. Review the experience the following week.

40. Facilitate group discussion about children's ongoing reactions to the divorce (e.g., asking questions over and over, easily becoming sad or mad, engaging in fantasy play).

41. Explore group members' reactions to their children's behavior from the perspective of the children's best interests, and help members develop strategies for reacting more appropriately.

42. Teach active listening and assertive communication skills, and practice using role plays and behavioral rehearsal.

__. _____

_____

__. _____

_____

__. _____

_____

DIAGNOSTIC SUGGESTIONS

Axis I:	309.0	Adjustment Disorder With Depressed Mood
	309.24	Adjustment Disorder With Anxiety
	309.28	Adjustment Disorder With Mixed Anxiety and Depressed Mood
	300.4	Dysthymic Disorder
	300.02	Generalized Anxiety Disorder
	296.xx	Major Depressive Disorder
	_____	_____
	_____	_____
Axis II:	301.6	Dependent Personality Disorder
	301.83	Borderline Personality Disorder
	301.81	Narcissistic Personality Disorder
	301.50	Histrionic Personality Disorder
	_____	_____
	_____	_____

SHYNESS

BEHAVIORAL DEFINITIONS

1. High levels of anxiety experienced in any social interaction situation.
2. Low frequency of dating.
3. In a social situation speaks few words, rarely initiates conversations, speaks softly, and has minimal or no eye contact.
4. Avoids social contact due to a self-perception of social inadequacy or lack of social skills.
5. Recalls negative experiences in social situations much more readily than positive experiences.
6. Recalls negative self-descriptions by others more readily than positive self-descriptions.
7. Pessimism about social situations in general, leading to an overestimation of the likelihood of unpleasantness in social interactions.
8. A pattern of dealing with threatening situations by rumination and worry.
9. Underestimation of own ability to cope with social situations.
10. Feelings of low self-esteem, in particular feelings of shame, accompanied by self-critical thoughts.

—. _____

_____

—. _____

_____

—. _____

_____

LONG-TERM GOALS

1. Increase the amount of time spent participating in social events.
2. Improve interpersonal communication skills.
3. Reduce physiological arousal in social situations.
4. Replace negative, self-critical cognitions with reality-based, self-affirming cognitions.
5. Increase active observation of others and attendance to others' emotional needs and personal desires, thereby decreasing self-focus.
6. Increase general optimism regarding the outcome of social interactions.
7. Improve feelings of self-esteem.

__. _____
  _____

__. _____
  _____

__. _____
  _____

SHORT-TERM OBJECTIVES

1. Each group member describe some of his/her negative experiences with and feelings about social interaction. (1)

2. Practice using a safe-place visualization when feeling anxious or unsafe. (2)

3. Verbalize understanding of the major components of social readiness; demonstrate them in the group first and later during *in vivo* social situations. (3)

4. Practice listening and public speaking skills by getting to know one member of

THERAPEUTIC INTERVENTIONS

1. Ask each group member to describe some of their most anxious moments in social interaction.

2. Lead a guided imagery of a safe place where group members can feel safe and relaxed.

3. Teach the acronym SOFTEN, which represents the elements of social readiness (*s*miling, *o*pen posture, *f*orward lean, *t*ouch, *e*ye contact, *n*odding), and have members present themselves accordingly to each other in dyads.

the group by questioning and then introducing him/her to the group. (4)

5. Accept appreciation for efforts made at listening and public speaking and give appreciation for support received. (5)

6. Increase knowledge of current events as a basis for social discourse. (6)

7. Verbalize understanding of the concept of the self-enhancement bias in attribution and how shy people tend to reverse that bias in attribution. (7)

8. Verbalize an understanding of how the reverse in the self-enhancement bias is related to childhood experiences of criticism, and identify experiences in own life. (8, 9)

9. Describe the negative cognitions that maintain the self-enhancement reversal. (10)

10. Verbalize increased awareness of the personal elements involved in social interactions: feelings, thoughts, and physiological responses. (11, 12)

11. Practice thought-stopping techniques on the negative cognitions that accompany social anxiety. (13)

12. Replace negative cognitions with reality-based, self-affirming cognitions. (14, 15, 16)

4. Have members spend 10 minutes in dyads, asking each other questions to get acquainted. Then have each person introduce their partner to the rest of the group.

5. Express (and encourage group members to express) support and appreciation for members' efforts at listening and public speaking.

6. Assign group members to read a newspaper or weekly newsmagazine to increase available topics of conversation.

7. Teach the concept of the typical self-enhancement bias in attribution, in which the average person blames the situation when something goes wrong and takes credit when things go well; describe how shy people tend to reverse that typical bias in attribution, blaming themselves when something goes wrong and giving credit to the situation when things go well.

8. Encourage group members to share examples of situations in which they have reversed the self-enhancement bias.

9. Elicit group members' early-childhood experiences of criticism that contribute to current negative cognitions and the self-enhancement reversal.

13. Write and articulate daily affirmations. (17, 18)

14. Expand personal repertoire of social behavior, making one specific behavioral change at a time. (19, 20)

15. Implement a system of reinforcement for new behaviors, using contingent preferred behaviors or tokens/money as rewards. (21)

16. Report a reduction in self-focus during social interactions accompanied by an increase in attendance to others. (22)

17. Demonstrate a willingness to persevere in social situations despite anxiety. (23)

18. Verbalize an understanding of the difference between relaxing and losing control. (24)

19. Practice progressive relaxation exercises and differential relaxation exercises to reduce the anxiety associated with social situations. (25, 26, 27, 28)

20. Practice using positive affirmations while doing relaxation exercises, ending the exercises with a visualization of social success. (29, 30)

21. Complete a systematic desensitization protocol toward a particular goal involving a successful social interaction. (31)

22. Report a reduction of anxiety when implementing so-

10. Facilitate discussion and identification of the current negative cognitions that maintain the self-enhancement reversal.

11. Have group members keep a social interaction diary during the week to record details of each social interaction, including what occurred, how they felt, what they said to themselves, and their concomitant physiological responses.

12. Have members report back to the group on their social interaction experiences during the week, using their diary material for reference.

13. Teach thought-stopping techniques (e.g., mentally shouting "Stop," wearing a rubber band around the wrist and snapping it), and encourage members to use them in social situations when they are aware of negative cognitions.

14. Ask each group member to write a list of 15 characteristics he/she likes about him/herself (e.g., "I'm generous, hardworking, have a good sense of humor . . ."). Then have each write a list of 10 things he or she does well.

15. Assist group members in using their lists to develop reality-based, self-affirming cognitions to substitute for negative cognitions, and encourage them to practice

cial interaction behavior listed in the systematic desensitization hierarchy. (32)

23. Verbalize an understanding of the elements of trust. (33, 34)

24. Describe the difficulty in letting oneself trust another. (34)

25. Describe how own behavioral responses (e.g. silence, laughing nervously) inhibit the development of trust with others, and identify changes that might be made to enhance trust. (35)

26. Demonstrate active listening skills and the use of "I" statements. (36, 37, 38)

27. Verbalize an understanding that different people have different perspectives of the same situation. (39)

28. Verbalize the difference between passive, aggressive, and assertive communication. (40)

29. Assertively communicate thoughts, feelings, and needs. (41)

30. Utilize assertiveness and problem-solving skills to deal with conflict. (40, 41, 42, 43)

31. Demonstrate healthy responses to criticism, including fogging, negative inquiry, and negative assertion. (44, 45)

these in conjunction with thought-stopping techniques. In particular, focus on changing global, stable cognitions to more-focused, transient cognitions. (e.g., "I can never assert myself with anyone" could be changed to "I was nervous in that situation and had a hard time asserting myself, but assertiveness is a skill and I am working on improving").

16. Assign group members to report back to the group on their success in replacing negative cognitions with positive cognitions; reinforce successes and confront catastrophizing of perceived failure.

17. Help members write some short, powerful, positive statements that can be used as daily affirmations to counter the negative cognitions (e.g., "I am a caring, sensitive person," "I work hard and am very efficient at what I do," "I am bright and curious"). Encourage them to repeat these affirmations several times each day.

18. Have members report back to the group on their success in using daily affirmations during the week; reinforce successes and hopeful statements regarding future performance in social situations.

—· _____
      _____
—· _____
      _____
—· _____
      _____

19. Ask group members to commit to trying one new social behavior during the week (e.g., making eye contact, initiating a conversation, sustaining a conversation, inviting someone over for coffee). Strategize a plan ahead of time in small groups.

20. Have members report back to the group on their success in trying a new social behavior during the week, including their thoughts throughout the process; encourage group members to reinforce each other for success and to offer suggestions for overcoming failures.

21. Assist group members in the development of a reward system, and encourage them to reward themselves with preferred behaviors or with tokens/money every time they behave in a new prosocial way, regardless of the outcome of the situation.

22. Assign group members to focus on the other person during a social interaction, keeping a mental record of the color of that person's eyes and hair, his/her facial expression, and what he/she may be feeling. Have members report their findings to the group.

23. Facilitate group members' exploration of the benefits

of continuing a social interaction despite anxiety, and
teach the process of using
information gathered from
the other person to keep a
conversation going.

24. Encourage group discussion
of the difference between
relaxing and losing control.
Explain that when begin-
ning relaxation exercises,
there may be enhanced
awareness of anxiety, but
that it dissipates with practice and does not indicate a
loss of control.

25. Teach progressive relaxation
exercises to the group, encouraging members to practice once or twice a day for
up to 30 minutes. Teach the
concept of SUDS (Subjective
Units of Distress scale) from
0 to 100 and have group
members rate their level of
anxiety before and after relaxation exercises.

26. Have members report back
to the group on their experience in doing the relaxation
exercises during the week,
reinforcing successes and
redirecting failures.

27. Use role play, behavior rehearsal, and modeling to
teach *differential relaxation,* or relaxation of only
those muscles not needed
during social interactions
(e.g., facial, hand, arm, and
shoulder muscles); encourage group members to practice during the week.

28. Have group members report on the *in vivo* practice of differential relaxation in social situations during the week; reinforce positive progress toward a sense of control over self.

29. Have group members practice relaxation using positive affirmations, repeating the affirmation with each exhalation.

30. Lead a guided positive visualization in which group members are enjoying social interactions, looking confident and happy; encourage members to practice this visualization at home after they use the relaxation exercises.

31. Teach the two steps of systematic desensitization: (1) construction of a hierarchy of increasingly anxiety-provoking situations; (2) visualization of the least anxiety-provoking situations, adding details to the visualization until SUDS levels reach 60 or above. Then instruct members to begin relaxing each muscle group until their SUDS levels are all below 30. Have them proceed through their hierarchies, reducing SUDS levels at each step until final goal is reached.

32. Assign group members, in small groups and then *in vivo*, to role-play their anxiety-provoking situations

while monitoring their SUDS levels. Remind members that the goal is to practice social interaction while relaxing.

33. Facilitate a discussion of the elements of trust in a group (honesty, self-disclosure, acceptance, careful listening, support, etc.).

34. Assign pairs of group members to go on a "trust walk," where one member leads a "blind" member (eyes closed or blindfolded) on a walk around the room. Each sighted leader helps the blind person explore the surroundings by using touch, sound, and smell. Process the blind members' difficulty in relinquishing control and trusting the partner.

35. Show group members how they might be perceived as more trustworthy (by making eye contact while listening, being more self-disclosing, etc.), and encourage group members to give feedback regarding these trust-inducing behaviors during interactions with other members.

36. Teach active listening skills, including (1) listening with full attention, (2) listening for the feelings as well as the content, and (3) paraphrasing to show the message has been heard. Have members practice the skills in small groups.

37. Teach the concept of "I" statements ("I feel _____ when you because _____"; "I would like _____"); have members practice in small groups.

38. Encourage the use of active listening skills and "I" statements during the week, and have members report back to the group on their experience, facilitating group members' reinforcement of each other's success.

39. Facilitate a group discussion about how messages are sent differently depending on the person's perspective and relationship with the listener. Have group members role-play being the sender and recipient in different scenarios (e.g., sharing a social success with a work colleague, another group member, or a critical parent). Then elicit the thoughts, feelings, and perspectives of each person involved in the scenario.

40. Teach the difference between passive (including passive-aggressive, a common style of shy people), aggressive, and assertive communication styles.

41. Use modeling, role playing, and behavior rehearsal to teach appropriate, assertive expression of a variety of feelings (frustration, anger, hurt, sadness, gratitude, joy, etc.), thoughts, and needs.

42. Teach the five steps to creative problem solving: (1) define the problem; (2) brainstorm possible solutions; (3) eliminate non-consensual solutions; (4) evaluate the pros and cons of the remaining possibilities and develop a plan of action; (5) evaluate the plan.

43. Have members appropriately and assertively express feelings of anger, and follow up with creative problem solving in role-play situations.

44. Teach three techniques of responding to criticism: (1) *fogging,* or agreeing that the criticism might be accurate, but asserting one's intention anyway (e.g., "I suppose you might be right that my shyness is all in my head, but I plan to continue working on my social skills at my own pace"); (2) *negative inquiry,* or asking the critic exactly what it is about one's behavior that the critic finds objectionable (e.g., "What exactly is it about my taking time to ask someone for a date that bothers you?"); and (3) *negative assertion,* or agreeing honestly with part or all of a criticism (e.g., "Yes, you're right. I did have a hard time focusing on what you were saying last night. When I get nervous that tends to happen. I

am working on being less self-focused"). Role-play real-life situations in small groups, and encourage members to implement during the week.

45. Have group members report on their experience in responding to criticism during the week; reinforce successful responding.

—. _____
   _____
—. _____
   _____
—. _____
   _____

DIAGNOSTIC SUGGESTIONS

Axis I: 300.23   Social Phobia
                300.00   Anxiety Disorder NOS
                300.4   Dysthymic Disorder

                _____   _____
                _____   _____

Axis II: 301.82   Avoidant Personality Disorder

                _____   _____
                _____   _____

SINGLE PARENTS

BEHAVIORAL DEFINITIONS

1. Sole or exclusive custody of child or children.
2. Greater than 50 percent custody of child or children following a divorce or separation.
3. Confusion and anxiety about how best to respond to the feelings of the children in adjusting to having only one parent living in the home.
4. Difficulty meeting own needs and desires in the face of child-rearing responsibilities.
5. Depression, anger, hurt, and guilt regarding not having a partner and having to parent alone.

__. _____
   _____

__. _____
   _____

__. _____
   _____

LONG-TERM GOALS

1. Consistently uphold the "best interests of the children" as paramount in making decisions about day-to-day life.
2. Balance own needs and desires with those of the children.
3. Mourn the lack of a partner and adjust to being a single parent.
4. Reduce feelings of depression, hurt, and anger.

—. _____
    _____
—. _____
    _____
—. _____
    _____

SHORT-TERM OBJECTIVES

1. Verbalize pressures of single parenting that precipitated joining group. (1)
2. Verbalize goals of participation in group. (2)
3. Describe the history of the relationship, including the break up, divorce, or death, which led to the present state of single parenthood. (3)
4. Give empathic support to, and accept same from, other group members. (4)
5. Describe the impact of single parenting on children and self in terms of social, intimate, and family relationships. (5, 6, 7)
6. List the rewards of single parenting versus shared custody. (8, 9)
7. Verbalize an understanding of the concept of "responsible selfishness" and how it can benefit own children. (10, 11)
8. Practice stress-reduction techniques to alleviate anxiety. (12, 13, 14)

THERAPEUTIC INTERVENTIONS

1. Each member introduce him/herself and describe the stressful incident that precipitated joining a single-parenting group.
2. Ask each member to articulate personal goals for participation in the group. Help group members assess the realistic nature of their goals.
3. Elicit from group members the personal histories of their relationships, including length of the relationship, number and ages of children, and the course of the relationship's ups and downs, culminating in the present state of single parenthood and the involvement of the ex-partner with his/her children.
4. Demonstrate, and encourage the group to provide, empathic support to the speaker.
5. Facilitate group sharing of the general effects of being a single-parent family.

9. Demonstrate time management and planning skills. (15, 16, 17, 20)

10. Share with other group members practical task and time management ideas that ease burden of single parenting. (17)

11. Increase frequency of self-nurturing activities. (18, 19, 20)

12. Identify distorted cognitions that contribute to depression, anxiety, and guilt. (21)

13. Replace distorted cognitions with realistic, self-affirming cognitions. (22, 23)

14. Report decrease in depression, anxiety, and guilt after using stress-reduction techniques and cognitive restructuring. (23)

15. Express feelings openly and honestly. (24, 25, 26)

16. Report decrease in angry feelings after using anger management tools. (26, 27, 28, 31)

17. Write letter (not to be mailed) to ex- or deceased partner expressing all the feelings associated with single parenting. (28, 29)

18. Demonstrate active listening skills and assertive communication skills. (30, 31, 32)

19. Report an increase in ability to ask for emotional support. (33, 34)

6. Have group members describe the specific effects of single parenting on the children and self in terms of social, intimate, and family relationships.

7. Brainstorm all the roles a single parent must take in keeping a household afloat (e.g., disciplinarian, cook, maid, nurse, teacher, nurturer, handyperson).

8. Facilitate group discussion of the rewards of single parenting versus shared custody for the parent (e.g., increased self-esteem, ability to make decisions without consultation, increased closeness with children, deeper communication with children), as well as its benefits for the children (e.g., consistent, predictable home life rather than moving back and forth between two homes, increased competence and self-reliance, increased closeness with custodial parent, deeper communication with parent).

9. Encourage members to compare the rewards inherent in their own situation with those of other group members.

10. Introduce to group members the concept of "responsible selfishness" (coined by Knight, author of *Enjoying Single Parenthood*), in which single parents must

20. Describe ongoing reactions of children to the single-parent environment, and report an increase in own ability to support children's feelings and needs. (35)

21. Increase participation in social activities to reduce social isolation. (36, 37)

22. List personal examples of guilt fostering a reluctance to adequately discipline the children, resulting in behavioral problems. (38, 39)

23. Report reduction in guilt feelings and discipline problems with children. (40, 41)

—. _____
   _____

—. _____
   _____

—. _____
   _____

put their own needs first at times to be able to best take care of their children.

11. Facilitate group sharing of ways in which their children would benefit from members putting their own needs ahead of those of their children.

12. Teach group members deep abdominal breathing and progressive relaxation skills to alleviate anxiety; encourage them to practice during the week.

13. Assist group members in developing general coping statements (e.g., "I am a competent parent"; "All parents have stress in dealing with children"; "I am just like others"; "Tomorrow will be a better day"; "Relax, this problem is not that critical").

14. Review group members' experiences in reducing anxiety by using deep breathing, progressive relaxation, and coping statements; reinforce successes and redirect failures.

15. Facilitate group discussion of general time management strategies, including the need for clarifying priorities.

16. Have members practice prioritizing their required tasks for the following week, making room for self-nurturing activities. Assist group members by encour-

aging their realistic expectations.

17. Encourage group exchange of practical task and time management ideas to ease the burden of single parenting and facilitate efficiency.

18. Assist group members in developing lists of self-nurturing activities that they could incorporate into their daily routines (e.g., soaking in a warm bath, reading a book, watching a movie).

19. Assign group members to use their time management strategies during the week, with particular attention to their prioritized list of tasks, including two or three self-nurturing activities each day.

20. Review group members' success using time management strategies that incorporate self-nurturing activities.

21. Help group members identify the negative, distorted cognitions that trigger feelings of depression, anxiety, and guilt.

22. Assist group members in developing realistic, self-affirming cognitions to replace negative self-talk, and encourage members to practice during the week.

23. Review members' experience in reducing depression, anxiety, and guilt by using

cognitive restructuring; reinforce successes and redirect unsuccessful attempts.

24. Encourage and reinforce
group members' open and
honest expression of feelings, in group and later
with significant others.

25. Explore with group members their fears of expressing anger, including the fear
of losing their children's affection.

26. Help members write out
their angry feelings before
communicating them to an-
other person.

27. Facilitate members' development of coping state-
ments to reduce anger (e.g.,
"I can stay calm and re-
laxed"; "Getting mad won't
help"); have them focus on
self-care instead.

28. Assign group members to
write a letter (not to be
mailed) to the ex- or de-
ceased partner expressing
all the feelings arising from
being a single parent.

29. Facilitate group discussion
of the experience of writing
a letter to the ex- or deceased partner.

30. Clarify the distinction between passive, passive-
aggressive, aggressive, and
assertive behavior.

31. Teach group members
active listening skills and
the use of assertive feeling statements (e.g., "I feel

_____ when you _____
because _____"; "I would
like _____").

32. Use role playing, modeling,
and behavioral rehearsal to
teach group members how
to implement active listening skills and make as-
sertive requests of their
dyad partners.

33. Assign group members to
use their assertive communication skills in asking for
emotional support *in vivo*
during the week.

34. Review group members'
success in asking for emotional support during the
week.

35. Have group members describe the ongoing reac-
tions of their children to the
single-parent environment.
Facilitate discussion about
how members can support
their children's feelings and
needs while not discounting
their own.

36. Assign group members to
participate in at least two
social activities each week
to reduce isolation. Solicit
from members a list of social resources for single parents, enhancing the list as
necessary.

37. Have members report back
to the rest of the group on
their participation in social
activities.

38. Explore with group members how guilt (over depriv-

ing their child of a second parent, not having enough time or energy for them, etc.) can interfere with the ability to discipline effectively by triggering a reluctance to set strict limits and follow through with appropriate consequences.

39. Elicit from group members their personal examples of difficulties in setting appropriate limits and consequences because of guilt. Explore the resulting behavioral problems of their children.

40. Help group members develop appropriate strategies (e.g., self-affirming cognitions, assertive communication) for reducing their guilt and resolving their children's discipline problems.

41. Review members' experiences in addressing their children's misbehavior, reinforcing successes and encouraging further strategizing in the case of failures.

__. _____
_____
__. _____
_____
__. _____
_____

DIAGNOSTIC SUGGESTIONS

Axis I: V62.89   Phase of Life Problem
          V61.20   Parent-Child Relational Problem
          _____   _____
          _____   _____

Axis II: V71.09   No Diagnosis on Axis II
          _____   _____
          _____   _____

TOXIC PARENT SURVIVORS

BEHAVIORAL DEFINITIONS

1. Self-report of childhood physical or emotional abuse or neglect in-flicted by a parent or parenting person who was chemically dependent, mentally ill, emotionally repressive, absent, or too busy.
2. Frequent conflicts within close friendships and intimate relationships.
3. Feelings of low self-esteem.
4. Irrational fears, suppressed rage, or identity conflicts related to painful early-life experiences.
5. Feelings of depression, anxiety, and loneliness.
6. Dissociative response to stressful situations.
7. Not actively suicidal or psychotic.
8. No history of substance abuse, or is in sustained full recovery from chemical dependence.
9. Concurrent participation in individual psychotherapy.

—. _____
   _____
—. _____
   _____
—. _____
   _____

LONG-TERM GOALS

1. Increase awareness of how childhood experiences have affected and continue to affect one's family life.
2. Develop awareness of the real, feeling self versus the adaptive self.

3. Spend more time in the real, feeling self without being emotionally overwhelmed.
4. Increase feelings of self-esteem.
5. Replace anger and depression with security and confidence.
6. Control the expression of feelings under stress.
7. Formulate goals for continuing work of recovery in individual therapy.

—. _____
   _____
—. _____
   _____
—. _____
   _____

SHORT-TERM OBJECTIVES

1. Describe the negative effects childhood abuse has had on behavior, thoughts, and feelings. (1)
2. Sign a confidentiality agreement. (2)
3. Articulate individual goals for group treatment of physical or emotional abuse or neglect. (3)
4. Practice self-calming exercises. (4, 5, 6)
5. Verbalize an increased awareness of the components of physical and emotional abuse and neglect. (7)
6. Describe what it was like to grow up in own family. (8)
7. Recognize and identify own childhood experiences as abusive. (9)

THERAPEUTIC INTERVENTIONS

1. Ask each group member to describe ways in which childhood experiences have affected her/him emotionally and behaviorally.
2. Have each group member sign confidentiality agreement in the presence of all other members.
3. Have group members state goals they would like to achieve while participating in the group.
4. Encourage members to monitor their levels of stress to avoid being flooded and emotionally shutting down.
5. Lead group members through a "safe-place" visualization (each member defining their own place where he/she can relax,

8. Increase tolerance for safe, nonthreatening, and nurturing hugs and other touches. (10, 11)

9. Monitor thoughts and feelings while in the process of recovery from abuse. (12, 13)

10. Identify the feelings about the abuser and other family members. (14, 15, 16)

11. Identify the complex feelings of guilt and shame toward self. (17)

12. Contrast the rules, rituals, and boundaries in functional families with the inconsistencies of own family. (18, 19)

13. Identify the role played within the family and the feelings associated with that role. (20, 21)

14. Verbalize the influence of childhood abuse experiences on present interactions. (22, 23, 24)

15. Identify any abusive patterns in own parenting. (25, 26, 27)

16. Verbalize an increased understanding of the concept of the "inner child" or "real self." (28, 29)

17. Differentiate between shame and guilt. (30)

18. Describe self using the negative, critical words used by abusive parent and by self as an adult; then contrast that with positive adjectives that could accurately describe self as a child and

trust, and feel accepted); encourage members to practice this visualization whenever stressed.

6. Ask group members to develop a nonverbal signal to indicate when their feelings are too intense and they need a time-out.

7. Define and describe the components of physical and emotional abuse and neglect. Stress the abusive effects of such "gray" or "innocuous" activities as corporal punishment, inadequate supervision, rejecting or withholding parenting, blaming or belittling, or observing another family member being abused.

8. Encourage group members to talk about their childhood experiences in broad terms, leaving the details for later.

9. Help group members recognize their experiences as abusive by identifying the impact of those experiences on current functioning. Encourage members to identify those elements of the speaker's story that resemble their own.

10. Explain to group members how "good" or safe, nurturing touches are important for emotional and physical well-being. Facilitate group discussion about each member's associations with touch.

later as an adult.
(31, 32, 33, 34, 35)

19. Decrease feelings of guilt and self-blame as manifested by an observed decrease in self-blaming statements and a reported decrease in self-blaming thoughts. (31, 32, 33, 34, 35)

20. Report a decrease in shameful feelings.
(30, 31, 32, 33, 34)

21. Identify own symptoms characteristic of Posttraumatic Stress Disorder. (36)

22. Verbalize an increased awareness of real feelings and personal desires.
(37, 38, 39, 40)

23. Demonstrate ability to express real feelings and then contain them as needed.
(40, 41)

24. Demonstrate assertiveness skills, including those needed in negotiating for personal needs and desires.
(42)

25. Assertively express anger in controlled, appropriate fashion. (42, 43, 44, 45)

26. Write a letter to abuser expressing various feelings that have resulted from the abuse. (46, 47)

27. Write a letter to nonprotective parent expressing feelings generated by the abuse. (48, 49)

28. Identify negative, critical cognitive distortions and

11. Encourage members to give therapist (and eventually each other) a supportive, friendly hug at the end of each group session. Give permission for members to participate or not based on their comfort level.

12. Assign group members to keep a journal documenting memories of their abuse, their current feelings about that abuse, and their strategies for coping with those feelings as children.

13. Ask members to keep a journal of their feelings regarding daily events, writing initially as though they are explaining the situation to someone else (e.g., "Every time I meet a new person I think I might like, I hear this voice telling me I'm ugly and no one will ever like me"). As they get stronger, have them write as if addressing the abuser (e.g., "You were always telling me how ugly I was and that no one would ever like me. I really resent how timid and insecure you've made me. In fact I hate you").

14. Explore with group members feelings about the abuse perpetrator, about the parent who did not protect them, and about what transpired when they told someone what had happened.

automatic thoughts about self. (50, 51, 52)

29. Practice thought-stopping techniques. (53)

30. Replace critical, abusive cognitions with realistic, self-affirming cognitions and logical comebacks. (54, 55)

31. Report a decrease in the use of dissociation as a response to stress. (56, 57)

32. Identify personal triggers of laughter as resource in self-nurturing. (58, 59)

33. Increase the frequency of self-nurturing behavior. (60)

__. _____
   _____

__. _____
   _____

__. _____
   _____

15. Model—and encourage group members to provide—supportive feedback.

16. Facilitate sharing by other members of similar experiences to those of the speaker.

17. Explore with group members the feelings of guilt ("I did bad things") and shame ("I am a bad person") resulting from childhood abuse.

18. Teach group members about family systems and the rules, rituals, and boundaries that provide stability and consistency in functional families.

19. Help group members identify the inconsistencies and unpredictability of their own family rules, rituals, and boundaries, and discuss the effects of such chaos on their current functioning.

20. Describe to group members the way children develop roles (e.g., the caregiver, the scapegoat, the rebel or "bad" child, the invisible, the mediator) to adapt to the dysfunctional demands of their families.

21. Elicit from group members personal examples of the roles adopted in their families and the feelings associated with those roles.

22. Facilitate group discussion of how roles that members adopted within the family serve them (or not) as adults.

23. Explore with group members current situations that remind them of the past.

24. Facilitate group discussion about how situations at work, with friends, or with family members can trigger old responses.

25. Explain to the group that people abused in childhood are at high risk for abusing their own children, but stress that seeking help is the first step toward changing that pattern.

26. Encourage group members to observe their parenting styles and identify similarities to those of their own, abusive parents.

27. Facilitate group discussion about members' observations of their own parenting styles.

28. Introduce the concept of the "inner child" or "real self" (that part of the self that is spontaneous, expressive, playful, creative, and instinctual) versus the adaptive self (who tends to adapt to what others expect).

29. Explore with the group the results of adapting to others' expectations (e.g., shutting off authentic feelings, eventually losing the ability to know what one is feeling altogether, emotional numbing).

30. Facilitate group discussion about the distinction be-

tween guilt (e.g., "I did something really bad") and shame (e.g., "I'm a really bad person").

31. Have group members write a list of the adjectives or phrases that their abusive parent would have used to describe them as children (selfish, stupid, a nuisance, etc.). Then have them write a list of how they would describe themselves as children (trying to be good, afraid, the caretaker, obedient, etc.).

32. Have group members write a list of adjectives or phrases describing themselves as adults (e.g., anxious, the caretaker, lonely) and another list of how they would like to be described (e.g., strong, nurturing, creative, healthy).

33. Facilitate members sharing their lists with the rest of the group.

34. Help members explore ways in which they already embody many of the qualities on their list of ideal characteristics.

35. Encourage members to confirm with other members the discrepancy between how they are now versus how they were perceived or described by their abusive parent.

36. Teach group members the symptoms of Posttraumatic

Stress Disorder (identifiable stressors, flashbacks, psychic numbing, and other symptoms such as hypervigilance, depression, anxiety, interpersonal difficulties, etc.). Have members compare their own symptoms with those described.

37. Help group members identify their feelings and needs by labeling them as they arise in discussions.

38. Have group members complete a word-association exercise, writing one, two, or three feelings in response to several words (e.g., *night, mother, father, dinnertime, birthday, holiday*). Distribute a list of common "feeling" words to facilitate identification of specific feelings.

39. Facilitate group discussion about the resistance shown by the adaptive self to acknowledging negative feelings.

40. Assign members to record in a journal feelings that arise during the week and share their experiences with the rest of the group.

41. Facilitate limited expression of real feelings by members, followed by their containment as needed to avoid flooding.

42. Teach assertive communication and problem-solving skills. Have group members practice expressing per-

sonal needs and desires in role plays.

43. Teach group members that experiencing and expressing anger is an important part of the grieving and recovery process.

44. Explore with the group the choices for handling anger learned as children (e.g., denying it and getting depressed; feeling but not expressing it; numbing it with drugs, alcohol, or food; or expressing it despite fearing punishment).

45. Using batakas and pillows or role-playing exercises, help group members safely express feelings of anger toward their abusive parent.

46. Assign group members to write a letter (not to be sent) to the abuser, expressing all the things they ever wanted to say to him/her.

47. Elicit members' responses to writing a letter to the abuser.

48. Assign group members to write a letter (not to be sent) to the parent who did not protect them.

49. Elicit members' responses to writing a letter to the nonprotective parent.

50. Help group members identify the negative automatic thoughts about self generated by their inner critical parent voice.

51. Teach the main categories of cognitive distortions. These include *all-or-nothing thinking* ("I blew it again, I'm a complete loser"); *overgeneralization* ("I can never get it right, nobody is ever going to like me"); *filtering* (not seeing the positive, only the negative); *disqualifying the positive* ("He's only saying that because he feels sorry for me"); *mind reading* ("She mustn't like me anymore"); *fortune-telling* (expecting the worst from every situation); and *catastrophizing* ("This is a disaster").

52. Elicit from group members personal examples of cognitive distortions from each category.

53. Teach thought-stopping techniques (e.g., snapping a rubber band worn around the wrist, mentally yelling "Stop"), and encourage group members to practice on their cognitive distortions.

54. Help group members develop some realistic, self-affirming cognitions as well as logical, positive comebacks to replace the cognitive distortions.

55. Encourage members to practice thought-stopping and to replace cognitive distortions with positive comebacks and self-affirming cognitions during the week

and report back on their success.

56. Teach group members about dissociation as a coping strategy for abuse survivors when under stress.

57. Help group members develop an awareness of their own tendency to dissociate, and encourage use of other strategies such as implementing time-out from stressful situations.

58. Assign members to find a cartoon, joke, or funny anecdote to share with the rest of the group. Have members rate their moods before and after the sharing of humorous material, and discuss how humor can be healing.

59. Facilitate exploration of what members find funny and what triggers their laughter. Assign them to watch a funny video during the week and rate their mood before and after.

60. Help members develop a list of self-nurturing behaviors (e.g., select from the *Inventory of Rewarding Activities* by Birchler and Weiss).

—. _____

_____

—. _____

_____

—. _____

_____

DIAGNOSTIC SUGGESTIONS

Axis I: 995.5   Physical Abuse of Child
               V61.21   Neglect of Child
               300.14   Dissociative Identity Disorder
               300.4   Dysthymic Disorder
               300.02   Generalized Anxiety Disorder

               _____   _____

               _____   _____

Axis II: 301.6   Dependent Personality Disorder
               301.82   Avoidant Personality Disorder
               301.83   Borderline Personality Disorder
               301.81   Narcissistic Personality Disorder

               _____   _____

               _____   _____

TYPE A STRESS

BEHAVIORAL DEFINITIONS

1. A pattern of pressuring self and others to accomplish more because it is believed that there is never enough time.
2. Tendency to become anxious or irritated when a person or situation does not conform to expectations.
3. A state of perpetual impatience with any waiting, delays, or interruptions.
4. Difficulty in sitting or doing nothing.
5. Almost all waking hours are consumed in work-related activity with little investment in relationships, recreation, or relaxation.

—. _____
   _____
—. _____
   _____
—. _____
   _____

LONG-TERM GOALS

1. Begin to formulate and implement a new life attitudinal pattern that allows for a more relaxing pattern of living.
2. Reach a balance between work and social time in daily life.
3. Achieve an overall decrease in compulsive, driven behaviors.
4. Begin to develop daily social and recreational routines.
5. Alleviate sense of time urgency, free-floating anxiety, and self-destructive behaviors.

—.   _____
     _____

—.   _____
     _____

—.   _____
     _____

SHORT-TERM OBJECTIVES

1. Verbalize current life stresses that precipitated participation in the group. (1)

2. Verbalize three general sources of stress, and give own examples that pertain to the three sources. (2, 3)

3. Verbalize an understanding of the impact of stress on the body. (4)

4. Identify and record own physiological concomitants to daily stress. (5, 6, 7)

5. Demonstrate the skill of deep abdominal breathing and progressive relaxation. (8, 9, 10, 11)

6. Report success at visualization of a safe place. (12, 13)

7. Identify obsessive anxiety- and general stress-provoking thoughts. (14)

8. Report reduction in anxiety- and general stress-provoking thoughts using thought-stopping techniques. (15, 16, 17)

THERAPEUTIC INTERVENTIONS

1. Ask each group member to introduce him/herself and describe the current life stresses that prompted participation in a stress management group.

2. Teach group members that stress results from changes (positive or negative) in one or more of the following: one's *environment* (e.g., noise, performance standards, time pressures, birth of a baby); one's *body* (e.g., aging, illness, injury, pregnancy, poor nutrition); one's *thoughts* (e.g., appraising or assessing a situation as difficult, dangerous, or painful).

3. Elicit from group members personal examples of the current stressors in their lives that result from changes in one's environment, body, or thoughts. Assign group members to complete the Holmes and Rahe stress chart to assist them in determining their recent stressors.

9. Verbalize the elements of Ellis and Dryden's ABCD model for disputing irrational thoughts. (18)

10. Demonstrate mastery of cognitive restructuring using the ABCD model. (19, 20, 21, 22)

11. Develop a hierarchy of stressful situations or events in daily life. (23)

12. Develop a personal list of coping statements relevant to hierarchy of stressful events. (26)

13. Report reduction in stress by applying relaxation techniques and coping statements to stressful events hierarchy, first using imagery and then *in vivo*. (24, 25, 27, 28)

14. Verbalize personal "bill of rights." (29)

15. Identify fears related to consequences of being assertive. (30)

16. Report a reduction in fear related to being assertive. (31, 35, 38)

17. Demonstrate active listening and assertiveness communication skills in group and with significant others. (32, 33, 34, 35)

18. Demonstrate assertive problem-solving skills in group and with significant others. (36, 37, 38)

19. Monitor time utilization for three days. (39, 40)

4. Describe the fight-or-flight response that occurs in reaction to a stressor and the long-term negative impact on the body of consistently high levels of stress (muscle myopathy, stress hypertension, peptic ulcers, colitis, etc.).

5. Lead group members through a body-awareness exercise, mentally scanning their bodies from head to toe to identify the muscle tension in different parts of their bodies.

6. Assign group members to monitor their physiological symptoms of stress by recording during the week stressful events, the time of their occurrence, and the physiological response associated with each event. Have members look for patterns in terms of particularly stressful times of day or characteristic responses to stress.

7. Review members' experiences of recording their stress symptoms; reinforce successes and redirect unsuccessful attempts.

8. Teach group members abdominal breathing, including breathing slowly and deeply into the abdomen, pausing, then exhaling completely.

9. Teach group members the progressive relaxation protocol, first tightening and

20. Identify period of maximum productivity. (41, 42)

21. Set realistic time priorities according to current goals. (43, 44, 45, 46)

22. Demonstrate success in time management and planning. (47, 48, 49)

23. Increase understanding of and commitment to good nutrition. (50)

24. Exercise aerobically at least four times per week for at least 20 to 30 minutes. (51, 52)

25. Identify and implement steps toward spiritual/meditative growth. (53, 54)

26. Increase the frequency of engaging in social/recreational activities with friends or family. (55, 56)

—. _____
   _____

—. _____
   _____

—. _____
   _____

then relaxing each muscle group from head to toe.

10. Have members practice abdominal breathing and progressive relaxation for 20 to 30 minutes per day and report back to the group the following week.

11. Review group members' experience with daily relaxation exercises; reinforce successes and gently confront failed attempts.

12. Guide group members through a safe-place visualization (e.g., a mountaintop, a private beach, or any other place where the member feels safe, comfortable, and in control), eliciting as much detail as possible.

13. Encourage group members to practice the visualization after doing the daily abdominal breathing and progressive relaxation protocol. Have members report back to the group on their success in practicing visualization.

14. Help group members identify their negative, anxiety-provoking and general stress-provoking cognitions.

15. Teach group members thought-stopping techniques (e.g., mentally shouting "Stop," snapping a rubber band worn around the wrist, redirecting thoughts to a more neutral focus) to reduce the impact of negative, anxiety-provoking cognitions.

16. Assign group members to practice thought-stopping techniques during the week.

17. Review group members' experiences of using thought-stopping techniques; reinforce successes and redirect unsuccessful attempts.

18. Teach Ellis and Dryden's ABCD model for disputing irrational thoughts, where A stands for the *activating* event, B is own *belief* system or thought about the event, C represents the *consequences* of A and B (the resulting feelings), and D stands for *disputing* the negative thoughts or beliefs and replacing them with positive, realistic beliefs.

19. Elicit from group members reality-based situations that consistently generate stressful emotions. Using the ABCD protocol, model the steps for disputing the associated irrational thoughts.

20. Have group members practice, in dyads, disputing the irrational thoughts associated with stressful events using the ABCD model.

21. Assign group members to practice, *in vivo*, using the ABCD model to challenge and replace irrational cognitions.

22. Review members' experiences of challenging and replacing irrational cognitions using the ABCD model. Re-

inforce successes and redirect negative experiences.

23. Describe to group members the process of stress inoculation (Meichenbaum and Cameron, 1974) in which one learns to relax in imagined scenes in anticipation of and preparation for real-life events. Encourage members to develop a personal hierarchy of stressful events or situations in daily life.

24. Instruct group members to visualize in detail the lowest item (event or situation) on their hierarchy of stress-related situations, and then guide them through deep-breathing and relaxation exercises until the item no longer triggers any stress or anxiety. Continue the exercise for each item in turn, progressing up the hierarchy.

25. Assign members to complete imagery desensitization of their hierarchies during the week, and report back to the group about their success.

26. Assist each group member in developing a personal list of coping statements that apply to his/her hierarchy of stressful events. Coping statements should address (1) preparation for the stressful event (e.g., "I've done this before, I can do it again," "There is no need to feel afraid," "It'll all be over

soon"), (2) facing the challenge of the event ("One
step at a time," "The best I
can do is good enough," "It's
okay to make a mistake"),
(3) feeling the fear arise
("Breathe the tension away,"
"I've survived this before,
and I will again now"), and
(4) self-congratulation
("Okay, it's over and I survived!").

27. Assign group members to
practice applying relaxation
techniques and coping
statements to *in vivo* stressful events.

28. Review group members' experiences of reducing their
stress by using coping statements and relaxation techniques. Reinforce successful
experiences and redirect
unsuccessful attempts.

29. Help members formulate a
list of their personal rights
(e.g., "You have the right to
say no," "You have the right
to make mistakes," "You
have the right to change
your mind") that facilitate
understanding of assertive
communication.

30. Elicit from group members
general fears about being
assertive (e.g., fear of rejection, fear of failure, fear of
making a fool of oneself).

31. Help members assess their
fears of being assertive in
specific situations and replace them with more adap-

tive feelings. Use specific questions to challenge these fears (e.g., "What is the worst thing that could happen?" "What belief triggers this fear?" "What evidence supports or refutes this belief?" "What might more realistically happen?" "What will happen if I keep doing as I have?").

32. Clarify the distinction between passive, aggressive, and assertive behavior.

33. Teach assertive communication skills, including active listening and "I" statements.

34. Have group members roleplay, in dyads, assertive responses to situations they are currently facing in their lives.

35. Assign group members to practice assertive expression of feelings, thoughts, and desires to others during the week and report back to the group at the next session.

36. Teach the five steps of assertive problem solving: (1) define the problem; (2) brainstorm possible solutions; (3) eliminate nonconsensual solutions; (4) evaluate the pros and cons of the remaining possibilities and develop a plan of action; (5) evaluate plan.

37. Using role play and behavioral rehearsal, have group members practice assertive

problem solving of reality-based situations.

38. Assign group members to practice assertive problem solving with significant others during the week and report back to the group on their experiences.

39. Assign group members to monitor every activity they engage in, noting the time taken for that activity in the periods from waking up through lunch, from the end of lunch through dinner, and from the end of dinner until going to sleep. Provide them with forms to help them keep this record for three days; then total the time spent in each of various categories (e.g., socializing at work, routine tasks at work, productive work, meetings, telephone calls, sports, hobbies, household tasks, shopping); finally, divide by three and find the average daily time for each activity.

40. Facilitate group discussion about the insights gained while monitoring time utilization. Explore with group members those categories in which they would like to spend less or more time.

41. Help group members identify their personal period of maximum productivity using their time use records.

42. Facilitate the development of strategies for group members to decrease or increase time spent in the desired categories.

43. Assist group members in developing lists of lifetime goals, one-year goals, and one-month goals.

44. Have members prioritize goals in each list as follows: more desired or essential (top drawer), important but can be temporarily delayed (middle drawer), and easily put off indefinitely (bottom drawer).

45. Using two essential goals from each list, assist group members in identifying the steps necessary for achieving those goals. Ensure that the steps are clear, realistic, and manageable.

46. Encourage group members to commit to addressing only top-drawer goals for one month before making a new list.

47. Assign group members to write daily to-do lists of everything they would like to accomplish each day, prioritizing each item as top, middle, or bottom drawer, and working their way down, addressing only top-drawer items until complete.

48. Teach group members the rules for making time necessary for completion of top- (and then middle-) drawer

items (saying no; banishing bottom-drawer items; building time into the schedule for interruptions, unforseen problems etc.; and setting aside time for relaxation).

49. Review members' experiences in completing their daily goals; reinforce successes and facilitate extra strategizing around failed attempts.

50. Facilitate group discussion of the impact of nutrition on stress, supplying additional information where necessary. Encourage members' commitment to good nutrition.

51. Teach group members the positive physiological and psychological impact of exercise (e.g., rapid metabolism of excess adrenaline and thyroxin in the bloodstream, enhanced oxygenation of blood and brain leading to improved concentration, production of endorphins, reduced insomnia, increased feelings of well-being, reduced depression).

52. Encourage group members to formulate exercise programs, building toward a goal of 20 to 30 minutes at least four times per week. Recommend *Exercising Your Way to Better Mental Health* (Leith).

53. Encourage group members to discuss the concept of

taking time to enrich the spiritual/meditative aspect of their life as a means of escaping from stress, setting priorities, and turning worries over to a higher power.

54. Assist members in identifying how each might strengthen his/her spiritual/meditative life (e.g., reserving time to reflect quietly on goals for life; engaging in prayer; attending religious worship; studying spiritual literature; walking alone in the woods or at the seashore). Assign each to implement actions to facilitate this growth; process results in the group.

55. Help members assess the lack of time given to light-hearted recreation with friends and/or family, pointing out the benefit of a life balanced with social/recreational activities as diversion from stress.

56. Assign each member to list three fun activities that he/she will engage in during the coming week with friends/family and report back to the group.

__. _____
_____

__. _____
_____

__. _____
_____

DIAGNOSTIC SUGGESTIONS

Axis I:

300.02	Generalized Anxiety Disorder
300.00	Anxiety Disorder NOS
309.24	Adjustment Disorder With Anxiety
309.0	Adjustment Disorder With Depressed Mood
309.28	Adjustment Disorder With Mixed Anxiety and Depressed Mood
309.3	Adjustment Disorder With Disturbance of Conduct
309.4	Adjustment Disorder With Mixed Disturbance of Emotions and Conduct
_____	_____
_____	_____

Axis II:

V71.09	No Diagnosis on Axis II
_____	_____
_____	_____

VOCATIONAL STRESS

BEHAVIORAL DEFINITIONS

1. Interpersonal conflict (perceived harassment, shunning, confrontation, etc.) with coworkers.
2. Feelings of inadequacy, fear, and failure secondary to severe business losses.
3. Fear of failure secondary to success or promotion that increases perceived expectations for greater success.
4. Rebellion against and/or conflicts with authority figures in the employment situation.
5. Recently fired or laid off.
6. Perceived or actual job jeopardy.
7. Complaints of job dissatisfaction related to employment responsibilities.
8. Feelings of anxiety and/or depression related to vocational situation.

__. _____
_____

__. _____
_____

__. _____
_____

LONG-TERM GOALS

1. Improve satisfaction and comfort surrounding coworker relationships.
2. Increase sense of confidence and competence in dealing with work responsibilities.

3. Be cooperative with and accepting of supervision or direction in the work setting.

4. Increase sense of self-esteem and elevation of mood in spite of unemployment.

5. Increase job security as a result of more positive evaluation of performance by supervisor.

6. Engage in job-seeking behaviors consistently and with a reasonably positive attitude.

7. Increase job satisfaction and performance due to implementation of assertiveness and stress management strategies.

8. Reduce anxiety and depression related to employment status and return to stabilized mood.

—. _____

_____

—. _____

_____

—. _____

_____

SHORT-TERM OBJECTIVES

THERAPEUTIC INTERVENTIONS

1. Verbalize recent job conflict/stress that precipitated participation in group. (1)

2. Describe history of conflict with supervisor or coworkers, and express feelings (anger, helplessness, and fear) associated with the conflict. (2, 3)

3. Verbalize impact of vocational stress on family life, in particular the impact on relationships with partner and children. (4)

4. List the maladaptive coping skills currently used to deal with the job stress. (5, 6, 7)

1. Ask each member to describe the current employment-related stresses or conflicts that prompted him/her to join the group.

2. Elicit from group members personal histories of conflict with supervisors or coworkers.

3. Encourage the appropriate expression of feelings (e.g., anger, helplessness, and fear) associated with the conflict.

4. Have group members describe the effects of the vocational stresses/job loss on their lives and on their rela-

5. Give and accept empathic support. (8)

6. Identify patterns of conflict with people outside the work setting that mirror those conflicts that occur on the job. (9)

7. Identify own role in and responsibility for the conflict. (10, 11)

8. Verbalize acceptance of responsibility for own behavior, feelings, and role in conflict. (10, 11, 12)

9. Identify behavioral strategies to reduce or resolve conflict with supervisor or coworkers. (13)

10. Implement behaviors that will reduce interpersonal conflict and promote harmony on the job. (14, 15)

11. Practice stress-reduction techniques to contain anxiety. (16, 17)

12. Identify negative, distorted cognitions underlying the feelings of anger, helplessness, and fear. (18)

13. Replace distorted cognitions with reality-based, self-affirming cognitions. (19, 20, 21)

14. Identify successful experiences in all areas of life to affirm new reality-based cognitions. (22, 23)

15. Identify classes, further instruction, or training that could enhance job skills and reduce stress. (24)

tionships with their partners and children.

5. Facilitate group sharing of the dysfunctional coping strategies currently employed to deal with the stresses (e.g., withdrawal, aggression, substance use).

6. Explore with group members how maladaptive solutions to problems (dysfunctional coping strategies) can become problems in themselves.

7. Evaluate members for substance abuse, depression, and so forth, and make appropriate referrals.

8. Model, facilitate, and reinforce the providing of empathic support by group members to each other.

9. Elicit from group members possible patterns of interpersonal conflict occurring *outside* the work setting that mirror job-related conflicts.

10. Help group members identify own role in and responsibility for the conflict.

11. Confront, and encourage other members to confront, speaker's projections of responsibility for own feelings and behavior onto others.

12. Reinforce group members' statements that demonstrate acceptance of responsibility for own behavior, feelings, and role in job conflict or job loss.

16. Commit to job-skill-enhancement strategies. (25)

17. Verbalize an objective understanding of the history of circumstances that culminated in being fired or laid off. (2, 26, 27)

18. State the meaning of work and its relationship to self-esteem. (28)

19. List alternative sources of self-esteem apart from vocation. (29)

20. Articulate difference between passive (including passive-aggressive), aggressive, and assertive behaviors. (30)

21. Demonstrate assertive skills, including active listening, "I" statements, and assertive problem solving. (31, 32, 33)

22. Demonstrate time management and planning skills. (34)

23. Verbalize comprehensive plan to search for a new job. (35, 36)

24. Verbalize any fear of failure and its precipitants. (37)

25. Identify the roots of fear of failure. (38)

26. Verbalize an understanding of the causes for and debilitating effects of fear of failure. (39)

27. Identify behavioral and cognitive strategies that will be used to overcome fear of failure. (40)

13. Facilitate group brainstorming of behavioral strategies (using "I" messages, apologizing for own part in the conflict, implementing reinforcement of supervisor's positive behaviors, etc.) to reduce or resolve conflict with supervisor or coworkers. Encourage members to identify similarities between own and speakers' experiences.

14. Assist group members in developing personal plans for using behavioral strategies *in vivo* to reduce or resolve job conflict.

15. Review members' experiences with behavioral strategies to reduce interpersonal conflict at work. Reinforce successes and encourage further strategizing in the face of failures.

16. Teach group members deep abdominal breathing and progressive muscle relaxation techniques to reduce stress and anxiety.

17. Encourage group members to practice deep abdominal breathing and progressive muscle relaxation on a daily basis. Review their experiences in the group, reinforcing successes and redirecting unsuccessful attempts.

18. Help group members identify negative, distorted cognitions that underlie the

—. _____

_____

—. _____

_____

—. _____

_____

job-related feelings of anger, helplessness, and fear.

19. Facilitate members' development of realistic, self-affirming cognitions to replace the negative, distorted self-statements.

20. Assign group members to practice *in vivo* replacing of negative, distorted cognitions with realistic, self-affirming cognitions.

21. Have members report back to the group on their experiences with cognitive restructuring; reinforce successes and restrategize failed attempts.

22. Elicit from group members successful experiences in areas of life outside of work (at home, with children, with partners, on leisure pursuits, in school, etc.).

23. Facilitate incorporation of group members' successful life experiences into positive affirmations, and encourage daily use.

24. Explore with group members the job-skill-enhancement resources available, including classes, computer-based training programs, written materials, and so forth.

25. Help group members evaluate own need for job-skill enhancement, and encourage commitment to appropriate strategies where relevant.

26. Facilitate members' realistic evaluation of their successes and failures on the job.

27. Assist group members in identifying the causes for own job jeopardy or termination that were outside their control.

28. Explore with group members the meaning of work in their lives (e.g., the basis of identity, sense of accomplishment, sense of purpose), and discuss why it contributes so profoundly to self-esteem.

29. Brainstorm with the group about sources of self-esteem unrelated to employment (meaningful relationships with intimates and children, friendships, hobbies, recreation, spiritual fulfillment, etc.).

30. Clarify the distinction between passive (including passive-aggressive), aggressive, and assertive behaviors.

31. Teach group members assertive communication skills, including active listening, assertive feeling statements (e.g., "I feel _____ when you _____ because _____"; "I would like _____"), and assertive problem solving (defining the problem, brainstorming possible solutions, evaluating and eliminating nonconsensual alternatives,

choosing a possible solution
and developing a plan, evaluating plan).

32. Use role playing, modeling,
and behavioral rehearsal to
teach group members the
implementation of active
listening skills, problem
solving, and making as-
sertive requests of their
dyad partners.

33. Assign members to use
their assertive communication skills *in vivo* during the
week and report back to the
group on their experiences.

34. Facilitate group discussion
of general time manage-
ment and planning strate-
gies (identifying priorities,
focusing on high-priority
items, saying no to low-
priority requests, etc.).

35. Help group members develop comprehensive plans
for a job search that contain
specific, realistic objectives
(e.g., looking at want ads,
rewriting—or seeking help
in writing—resumes, talk-
ing to friends, family, and
colleagues about job opportunities).

36. Elicit commitment from
group members to follow
plans for conflict resolution
or job search.

37. Ask members to acknowledge any fear of failure that
is associated with current
success or with the need to
initiate new, risky behav-

iors (e.g., job search, new job responsibilities, change of job performance due to job jeopardy).

38. Explore with group members the roots of fear of failure (e.g., past vocational setbacks or disappointments, critical family of origin experiences, lack of support from current social network).

39. Teach group members how fear of failure is based in dysfunctional cognitive messages and often results in a paralyzing of abilities that becomes a self-fulfilling prophecy of failure.

40. Assist members in devising strategies to overcome fear of failure (e.g., implementing positive self-talk, realistically acknowledging successes from the past, soliciting support from significant others, separating past family of origin criticisms of self from current situation). Elicit commitment from group members to pursue strategies.

__. _____
    _____

__. _____
    _____

__. _____
    _____

DIAGNOSTIC SUGGESTIONS

Axis I: 309.24   Adjustment Disorder With Anxiety
              309.0   Adjustment Disorder With Depressed Mood
              309.28   Adjustment Disorder With Mixed Anxiety and
                          Depressed Mood
              300.4   Dysthymic Disorder
              300.02   Generalized Anxiety Disorder
              V62.2   Occupational Problem

              _____   _____

              _____   _____

Axis II: 301.0   Paranoid Personality Disorder
              301.6   Dependent Personality Disorder
              301.81   Narcissistic Personality Disorder
              301.82   Avoidant Personality Disorder
              301.9   Personality Disorder NOS
              301.7   Antisocial Personality Disorder

              _____   _____

              _____   _____

Appendix A

BIBLIOTHERAPY SUGGESTIONS

Adult Children of Alcoholics

Beattie, M. (1987). *Codependent No More*. San Francisco: Harper.
Black, C. (1980). *It Will Never Happen to Me*. Denver: MAC Publishing.
Cermak, T. L. (1988). *A Time to Heal*. New York: Avon Books.
Schaef, A. W. (1986). *Co-dependence*. San Francisco: Harper & Row.
Woititz, J. (1990). *Adult Children of Alcoholics*. Deerfield Beach, FL: Health Communications, Inc.

Agoraphobia

Bourne, E. (1995). *The Anxiety & Phobia Workbook*. 2d ed. Oakland, CA: New Harbinger.
Leith, L. M. (1998). *Exercising Your Way to Better Mental Health*. Morgantown, WV: Fit Information Technology, Inc.
Weekes, C. (1976). *Simple, Effective Treatment of Agoraphobia*. New York: Bantam Books.

Anger Control

McKay, M., P. D. Rogers, and J. McKay (1989). *When Anger Hurts*. Oakland, CA: New Harbinger.
McKay, M., K. Paleg, P. Fanning, and D. Landis (1996). *When Anger Hurts Your Kids*. Oakland, CA: New Harbinger.
Potter-Efron, R. (1994). *Angry All the Time*. Oakland, CA: New Harbinger.
Tavris, C. *Anger: The Misunderstood Emotion*. New York: Touchstone.

Anxiety

Benson, H. (1975). *The Relaxation Response*. New York: William Morrow.
Bourne, E. (1998). *Healing Fear*. Oakland, CA: New Harbinger.
Burns, D. (1993). *Ten Days to Self-Esteem*. New York: William Morrow.
Craske, M., and D. Barlow (1994). *Mastering Your Anxiety and Panic—Patient's Workbook*. San Antonio, TX: The Psychological Corporation.
Davis, M., E. Eshelman, and M. McKay (1988). *The Relaxation and Stress Reduction Workbook*. Oakland, CA: New Harbinger.

Leith, L. M. (1998). *Exercising Your Way to Better Mental Health.* Morgantown, WV: Fit Information Technology, Inc.

Zuercher-White, E. (1998). *An End to Panic.* Oakland, CA: New Harbinger.

Assertiveness Deficit

Alberti, R. E., and M. Emmons (1974). *Your Perfect Right.* San Luis Obispo, CA: Impact Press.

Bloom, L. Z., K. Coburn, and J. Pealman (1976). *The New Assertive Woman.* New York: Addison-Wesley.

Smith, M. (1975). *When I Say No, I Feel Guilty.* New York: The Dial Press.

Bulimia

Chernin, K. (1981). *The Obsession.* New York: Harper & Row.

Hollis, J. (1985). *Fat Is a Family Affair.* New York: Harper & Row.

Orbach, S. (1978). *Fat Is a Feminist Issue.* New York: Berkley.

Sandbek, T. J. (1986). *The Deadly Diet.* Oakland, CA: New Harbinger.

Caregiver Burnout

Becker, M. R. (1993). *Last Touch.* Oakland, CA: New Harbinger.

Daniel, J. (1996). *Looking After.* Washington, DC: Counterpoint.

Levin, N. J. (1997). *How to Care For Your Parents.* New York: Norton.

Mace, N. L., and P. V. Rabins (1981). *The 36-Hour Day.* Baltimore: The Johns Hopkins University Press.

Chemical Dependence

Alcoholics Anonymous (1976). *Alcoholics Anonymous: The Big Book.* New York: A. A. World Service.

Fanning, P., and J. O'Neill (1996). *The Addiction Workbook.* Oakland, CA: New Harbinger.

Johnson, V. (1980). *I'll Quit Tomorrow.* New York: Harper & Row.

Wegscheider-Cruse, S. (1989). *Another Chance: Hope and Health for the Alcoholic Family.* 2d ed. Palo Alto, CA: Science and Behavior Books, Inc.

Child Molester—Adolescent

Donaforte, L. (1982). *I Remembered Myself: The Journal of a Survivor of Childhood Sexual Abuse.* Ukiah, CA: self-published.

Chronic Pain

Catalano, E. M., and K. N. Hardin (1996). *The Chronic Pain Control Workbook.* Oakland, CA: New Harbinger.

Davis, M., E. R. Eshelman, and M. McKay (1995). *The Relaxation and Stress Reduction Workbook.* Oakland, CA: New Harbinger.

Codependence

Beattie, M. (1987). *Codependent No More*. San Francisco: Harper.
Bradshaw, J. (1988). *Healing the Shame That Binds You*. Deerfield Beach, FL: Health Communications.
Schaef, A. W. (1986). *Co-Dependence*. San Francisco: Harper & Row.

Depression

Burns, D. D. (1980). *Feeling Good: The New Mood Therapy*. New York: Signet.
Burns, D. D. (1989). *The Feeling Good Handbook*. New York: Plume.
Copeland, M. E. (1992). *The Depression Workbook*. Oakland, CA: New Harbinger.
Leith, L. M. (1998). *Exercising Your Way to Better Mental Health*. Morgantown, WV: Fit Information Technology, Inc.
Mcdina, J. (1998). *Depression*. Oakland, CA: New Harbinger.

Domestic Violence Offenders

Martin, D. (1976). *Battered Wives*. New York: Pocket Books.
McKay, M., P. D. Rogers, and J. McKay (1989). *When Anger Hurts*. Oakland, CA: New Harbinger.

Domestic Violence Survivors

Betancourt, M., and R. E. McAfee (1997). *What to Do When Love Turns Violent: A Practical Resource for Women in Abusive Relationships*. New York: Harper Perennial Library.
Deschner, J. P. (1984). *How to End the Hitting Habit*. New York: The Free Press.
Ens, G., and J. Black (1997). *It's Not Okay Anymore*. Oakland, CA: New Harbinger.
Jacobson, N. S., and J. M. Gottman (1998). *When Men Batter Women: New Insights into Ending Abusive Relationships*. New York: Simon & Schuster.
Martin, D. (1976). *Battered Wives*. New York: Pocket Books.
Paleg, K. (1989). "Spouse Abuse." In McKay, M., P. D. Rogers, and J. McKay, *When Anger Hurts*. Oakland, CA: New Harbinger.

Grief/Loss Unresolved

Colgrove, M., H. H. Bloomfield, and P. McWilliams (1976). *How to Survive the Loss of a Love*. New York: Bantam Books.
Finkbeiner, A. K. (1996). *After the Death of a Child: Living with Loss Through the Years*. New York: Free Press.
Schiff, H. S. (1978). *The Bereaved Parent*. New York: Viking Penguin.
Smedes, L. B. (1990). *Forgive and Forget*. New York: Pocket Books.
Staudacher, C. (1987). *Beyond Grief*. Oakland, CA: New Harbinger.
Zonnebelt-Smeenge, S. J., and R. C. DeVries (1998). *Mourning into Dancing: Getting to the Other Side of Grief*. Ada, MI: Baker Books.

HIV/AIDS

Gifford, A. L., K. Lorig, D. Laurent, and V. Gonzalez (1997). *Living Well with HIV and AIDS.* Palo Alto, CA: Bull.

Klitzman, R. (1997). *Being Positive.* Chicago: Ivan R. Dee.

Smedes, L. B. (1990). *Forgive and Forget.* New York: Pocket Books.

Staudacher, C. (1987). *Beyond Grief.* Oakland, CA: New Harbinger.

Incest Offenders (Adult)

Donaforte, L. (1982). *I Remembered Myself: The Journal of a Survivor of Childhood Sexual Abuse.* Ukiah, CA: self-published.

Forward, S., and C. Buck (1988). *Betrayal of Innocence: Incest & Its Devastation.* New York: Viking Penguin.

Herman, J. (1982). *Father-Daughter Incest.* Cambridge, MA: Harvard University Press.

Incest Survivors (Adult)

Bass, E., and L. Davis (1988). *The Courage to Heal: A Guide for Women Survivors of Child Sexual Abuse.* San Francisco: HarperCollins.

Bradshaw, J. (1988). *Healing the Shame That Binds You.* Deerfield Beach, FL: Health Communications, Inc.

Davis, L. (1990). *The Courage to Heal Workbook: For Men and Women Survivors of Child Sexual Abuse.* San Francisco: HarperCollins.

Gil, E. (1984). *Outgrowing the Pain.* New York: Dell Publishing.

McKay, M., and P. Fanning (1992). *Self-Esteem.* Oakland, CA: New Harbinger.

Infertility

Cooper, S. L., and E. S. Glazer (1994). *Beyond Infertility.* New York: Lexington Books.

Friedman, J. S. (1995). *How to Become Your Own Best Infertility Counselor: Helping You Understand Your Struggle; Deciding What's Best for You, and Educating Others to Accept Your Choice.* Fort Thomas, KY: Jolance Press.

Goldfarb, H. A. (1995). *Overcoming Infertility: 12 Couples Share Their Success Stories.* New York: John Wiley & Sons.

Peoples, D. (1998). *What to Expect When You're Experiencing Infertility: How to Cope with the Emotional Crisis and Survive.* New York: Norton.

Parenting Problems

Dinkmeyer, D., and D. G. McKay (1983). *The Parent's Guide: Systematic Training for Effective Parenting of Teens.* Circle Pines, MN: American Guidance Service.

Faber, A., and E. Mazlish (1987). *Siblings Without Rivalry.* New York: Norton.

Fleming, D. (1989). *How to Stop the Battle with Your Teenager.* New York: Prentice Hall.

Paleg, K. (1997). *The Ten Things Every Parent Needs to Know.* Oakland, CA: New Harbinger.

Pantley, E. (1996). *Kid Cooperation.* Oakland, CA: New Harbinger.

Pryor, K. (1984). *Don't Shoot the Dog.* New York: Bantam Books.

Phobias—Specific/Social

Bourne, E. (1995). *Anxiety and Phobia Workbook.* 2d ed. Oakland, CA: New Harbinger.

Burns, D. (1993). *Ten Days to Self-Esteem.* New York: William Morrow.

Leith, L. M. (1998). *Exercising Your Way to Better Mental Health.* Morgantown, WV: Fit Information Technology, Inc.

Swede, S., and S. Jaffe (1987) *The Panic Attack Recovery Book.* New York: New American Library.

Rape Survivors

Adams, C., and J. Fay (1989). *Free of the Shadows.* Oakland, CA: New Harbinger.

Benedict, H. (1985). *Recovery: How to Survive Sexual Assault for Women, Men, Teenagers, and Their Friends and Family.* New York: Doubleday and Co.

Katz, J. H. (1984). *No Fairy Godmothers, No Magic Wands: The Healing Process After Rape.* Saratoga, CA: R & E.

Matsakis, A. (1996). *I Can't Get Over It.* Oakland, CA: New Harbinger.

Warshaw, R. (1988). *I Never Called It Rape: The Ms Report on Recognizing, Fighting, and Surviving Date and Acquaintance Rape.* New York: Harper & Row.

Separation and Divorce

Gardner, R. A. (1991). *The Parent's Book About Divorce.* New York: Bantam Books.

McKay, M., P. D. Rogers, J. Blades, and R. Gosse (1984). *The Divorce Book.* Oakland, CA: New Harbinger.

Ricci, I. (1997). *Mom's House, Dad's House.* New York: Fireside.

Shyness

Cheek, J. M. (1989). *Conquering Shyness.* New York: Basic Books.

Gabor, D. (1983). *How to Start a Conversation and Make Friends.* New York: Fireside Books.

McKay, M., and P. Fanning (1992). *Self-Esteem.* Oakland, CA: New Harbinger.

Smith, M. J. (1975). *When I Say No, I Feel Guilty.* New York: Bantam Books.

Zimbardo, P. G. (1977). *Shyness: What It Is, What to Do About It.* Reading, MA: Addison-Wesley.

Single Parents

McKay, M., and P. Fanning (1997). *The Daily Relaxer.* Oakland, CA: New Harbinger.

McKay, M., P. D. Rogers, J. Blades, and R. Gosse (1984). *The Divorce Book.* Oakland, CA: New Harbinger.

Ricci, I. (1997). *Mom's House, Dad's House.* New York: Fireside.

Toxic Parent Survivors

Bradshaw, J. (1990). *Homecoming.* New York: Bantam Books.

Brown, E. M. (1989). *My Parent's Keeper.* Oakland, CA: New Harbinger.

Powell, J. (1969). *Why I'm Afraid to Tell You Who I Am.* Allen, TX: Argus Communications.

Whitfield, C. (1987). *Healing the Child Within.* Deerfield Beach, FL: Health Communications, Inc.

Type A Stress

Friedman, M., and D. Olmer (1984). *Treating Type A Behaviors and Your Heart.* New York: Alfred Knopf.

Leith, L. M. (1998). *Exercising Your Way to Better Mental Health.* Morgantown, WV: Fit Information Technology, Inc.

McKay, M., and P. Fanning (1997). *The Daily Relaxer.* Oakland, CA: New Harbinger.

O'Hara, V. (1996). *Five Weeks to Healing Stress.* Oakland, CA: New Harbinger.

Robinson, B. (1993). *Overdoing It.* Deerfield Beach, FL: Health Communications, Inc.

Vocational Stress

Bolles, R. (1992). *What Color Is Your Parachute?* Berkeley, CA: Ten Speed Press.

Jandt, F. (1985). *Win-Win Negotiating: Turning Conflict into Agreement.* New York: John Wiley & Sons.

O'Hara, V. (1995). *Wellness at Work.* Oakland, CA: New Harbinger.

Potter-Efron, R. (1998). *Working Anger.* Oakland, CA: New Harbinger.

Weiss, R. (1990). *Staying the Course: The Emotional and Social Lives of Men Who Do Well at Work.* New York: Free Press.

Appendix B

INDEX OF DSM-IV CODES ASSOCIATED WITH PRESENTING PROBLEMS

Amphetamine Abuse   305.70
   HIV/AIDS

Amphetamine Dependence   304.40
   HIV/AIDS

**Antisocial Personality
Disorder**   301.7
   Anger Control
   Assertiveness Deficit
   Chemical Dependence
   Domestic Violence Offenders

Anxiety Disorder NOS   300.00
   Adult Children of Alcoholics
   Anxiety
   Assertiveness Deficit
   Shyness
   Type A Stress

**Avoidant Personality
Disorder**   301.82
   Adult Children of Alcoholics
   Assertiveness Deficit
   Depression
   Incest Survivors—Adult
   Shyness
   Toxic Parent Survivors
   Vocational Stress

Bereavement   V62.82
   Grief/Loss Unresolved
   HIV/AIDS

Bipolar I Disorder   296.xx
   Anger Control

**Borderline Personality
Disorder**   301.83
   Anger Control
   Domestic Violence Offenders
   Incest Offenders—Adult
   Incest Survivors—Adult
   Separation and Divorce
   Toxic Parent Survivors

Bulimia Nervosa   307.51
   Bulimia

Cannabis Abuse   305.20
   Chemical Dependence

Cannabis Dependence   304.30
   Chemical Dependence

**Child or Adolescent
Antisocial Behavior**   V71.02
   Parenting Problems

Cocaine Abuse   305.60
   Chemical Dependence
   HIV/AIDS

Cocaine Dependence   304.20
   Chemical Dependence
   HIV/AIDS

Conduct Disorder   312.8x
   Child Molester—Adolescent

**Conduct Disorder/Adolescent
Onset Type**   312.82
   Anger Control

**Conduct Disorder/Childhood
Onset Type**   312.81
   Anger Control

**Dependent Personality
Disorder**   301.6
   Adult Children of Alcoholics
   Agoraphobia
   Bulimia
   Codependence
   Domestic Violence Survivors
   Incest Survivors—Adult
   Separation and Divorce
   Toxic Parent Survivors
   Vocational Stress

Depressive Disorder NOS   311
   Adult Children of Alcoholics
   Codependence
   Depression

Dissociative Disorder NOS 300.15
   Incest Survivors—Adult

**Dissociative Identity
Disorder**   300.14
   Toxic Parent Survivors

Practice Planners™ offer mental health
professionals a full array of practice management tools. These easy-to-use resources
include *Treatment Planners*, which cover

Practice *Planners*™

all the necessary elements for developing formal treatment plans, including detailed problem definitions, long-term goals, short-term objectives, therapeutic interventions, and DSM-IV diagnoses;
Homework Planners featuring behaviorally-based, ready-to-use assignments which are designed for
use between sessions; and *Documentation Sourcebooks* that provide all the forms and records that
therapists need to run their practice.

For more information on the titles listed below, fill out and return this form to: John Wiley & Sons, Attn: M.Fellin,
605 Third Avenue, New York, NY 10158.

Name _____

Address _____

Address _____

City/State/Zip _____

Telephone _____ Email _____

Please send me more information on:

❑   The Child and Adolescent Psychotherapy Treatment Planner / 240pp / 0-471-15647-7 / $39.95

❑   The Chemical Dependence Treatment Planner / 208pp / 0-471-23795-7 / $39.95

❑   The Continuum of Care Treatment Planner / 208pp / 0-471-19568-5 / $39.95

❑   The Couples Therapy Treatment Planner / 208pp / 0-471-24711-1 / $39.95

❑   The Employee Assistance (EAP) Treatment Planner / 176pp / 0-471-24709-X / $39.95

❑   The Pastoral Counseling Treatment Planner / 208pp / 0-471-25416-9 / $39.95

❑   The Older Adult Psychotherapy Treatment Planner / 176pp / 0-471-29574-4 / $39.95

❑   The Behavioral Medicine Treatment Planner / 176pp / 0-471-31923-6 / $39.95

❑   The Complete Adult Psychotherapy Treatment Planner, Second Edition / 224pp / 0-471-31922-4 / $39.95

❑   The Brief Couples Therapy Homework Planner / 224pp / 0-471-29511-6 / $49.95

❑   The Brief Therapy Homework Planner / 256pp / 0-471-24611-5 / $49.95

❑   The Chemical Dependence Treatment Homework Planner / 300pp / 0-471-32452-3 / $49.95

❑   The Adolescent Homework Planner / 256pp / 0-471-34465-6 / $49.95

❑   The Child Homework Planner / 256pp / 0-471-32366-7 / $49.95

❑   The Couples & Family Clinical Documentation Sourcebook / 208pp / 0-471-25234-4 / $49.95

❑   The Psychotherapy Documentation Primer / 224pp / 0-471-28990-6 / $39.95

❑   The Clinical Documentation Sourcebook / 256pp / 0-471-17934-5 / $49.95

❑   The The Forensic Documentation Sourcebook / 224pp / 0-471-25459-2 / $75.00

❑   The Chemical Dependence Treatment Documentation Sourcebook / 304pp / 0-471-31285-1 / $49.95

❑   The Child Clinical Documentation Sourcebook / 256pp / 0-471-29111-0 / $49.95

Order the above products through your local bookseller, or by
calling 1-800-225-5945, from 8:30 a.m. to 5:30 p.m., EST. You can
also order via our web site: www.wiley.com/practiceplanners

WILEY
Publishers Since 1807

ABOUT THE DISK*

TheraScribe® 3.0 and 3.5 Library Module Installation

The enclosed disk contains files to upgrade your TheraScribe® 3.0 or 3.5 program to include the behavioral definitions, goals, objectives, interventions, and diagnoses from *The Group Therapy Treatment Planner.*

Note: You must have TheraScribe® 3.0 or 3.5 for Windows installed on your computer to use *The Group Therapy Treatment Planner* library module.

To install the library module, please follow these steps:

1. Place the library module disk in your floppy drive.
2. Log in to TheraScribe® 3.0 or 3.5 as the Administrator using the name "Admin" and your administrator password.
3. On the Main Menu, press the "GoTo" button, and choose the Options menu item.
4. Press the "Import Library" button.
5. On the Import Library Module screen, choose your floppy disk drive a:\ from the list and press "Go." Note: It may take a few minutes to import the data from the floppy disk to your computer's hard disk.
6. When the installation is complete, the library module data will be available in your TheraScribe® 3.0 or 3.5 program.

Note: If you have a network version of TheraScribe® 3.0 or 3.5 installed, you should import the library module one time only. After importing the data, the library module data will be available to all network users.

User Assistance

If you need assistance using this TheraScribe® 3.0 or 3.5 add-on module, contact Wiley Technical Support at:

Phone: 212-850-6753
Fax: 212-850-6800 (Attention: Wiley Technical Support)
E-mail: techhelp@wiley.com

---

*Note: This section applies only to the book with disk edition, ISBN 0-471-25468-1.

For information on how to install disk, refer to the **About the Disk** section on page 303.

WILEY
Publishers Since 1807
